Returning to Seneca Falls

RETURNING TO SENECA FALLS

The First
Woman's Rights Convention
& Its Meaning
for Men & Women Today

BRADFORD MILLER

LINDISFARNE PRESS

Library of Congress Cataloging-in-Publication Data

Miller, Bradford, 1946–
    Returning to Seneca Falls : The first Woman's Rights
Convention and its meaning for men and women today /
Bradford Miller.
        p. cm.
    Includes bibliographical references.
    ISBN 0-940262-71-1 (pbk.)
    1. Woman's Right's Convention (1st : 1848 : Seneca Falls,
N.Y.) 2. Stanton, Elizabeth Cady, 1815-1902. 3. Douglass,
Frederick, 1817?-1895 — Contributions in woman's rights.
4. Women's rights — New York (State) — Seneca Falls —
History. 5. Men — New York (State) — Seneca Falls —
Psychology. 6. Feminism — New York (State) — Seneca Falls
— Philosophy. I. Title.
HQ1418.M55 1995
305.42'09747'69 — dc20   94-46571
                                                             CIP

Book design by Studio 31

Cover: the photograph of the author is by William Gibson; the
image of Frederick Douglass is from a daguerrotype c. 1850–1855
(collection of William Rubel); the image of Elizabeth Cady Staton
is a detail from a photograph c. 1855 (from the collection of Rhoda
Barney Jenkins.)

10 9 8 7 6 5 4 3 2 1

Printed in the United States of America

96 (? ? ?

CONTENTS

I will be sad to see the trees & birds on fire   Surely they are innocent as none of us has been

With their songs, they know the sacred   I am in a circle with that soft, enduring word

In it is the wisdom of all peoples   Without a deep, deep understanding of the sacredness of life, the fragility of each breath, we are lost   The holocaust has already occurred What follows is only the burning brush   How my heart aches & cries to write these words   I am not as calmly indifferent as I sound . . .

Chrystos, from "No Rock Scorns Me as Whore," *This Bridge Called My Back*

To Anna
with love, and to the family
we have made

Acknowledgments

James Hillman saw promise in my manuscript in its early stages, and was significantly encouraging. Donald Junkins of the University of Massachusetts' English Department offered fundamental guidance. The Northfield Mount Hermon School provided summer grants which helped support this project. Christopher Bamford's uncanny, patient, artistic leadership was instrumental throughout.

CHAPTER ONE

Orienteering

Not long ago, while white men bonded and beat drums in forest groupings, I wrestled with two figures that I feared would destroy me or, I supposed, give me birth. These two were the black male Frederick Douglass and the feminist female Elizabeth Cady Stanton, a man and a woman who survive in the shadows of the history of my home town of Seneca Falls, New York. In addition to their historic participation in the First Woman's Rights Convention at Seneca Falls in 1848, these two are also characters in the latent story of America that is somehow always emerging on this continent as the nerve pattern of a distinctly American consciousness. The story of Frederick Douglass and Elizabeth Cady Stanton crystallizes and animates the story of democracy itself, a vision in which men and women will free themselves to choose the opportunity of individual responsibility and self-realization, setting aside the child's play of prejudice and the bitter politics of race and gender.

Most men and women have not even heard of Seneca Falls or the mythic event that took place there. They may have learned in a historical sense that the First Woman's Rights Convention took place in Seneca Falls in 1848, but few are aware of its significance as the modern flashpoint in redefining the intellectual, emotional, and spiritual basis on which men and women will live for centuries to come.

It is in the afterglow of that event — sparked by Elizabeth Cady Stanton with the support of Frederick Douglass, the only man to speak in favor of her resolution demanding women's right to vote — that we can discern a new American map for the lives of women and men. I believe that if we understand these events we will be charged like iron filings being brought closer and closer to a magnet, the soul magnet of Seneca Falls.

I happen to be a man from Seneca Falls, and in what follows I think out loud, as it were, about what it means to be a male from this essentially women's place. As women struggle to define themselves intellectually, politically, emotionally, and spiritually, and as oppressed peoples, whether they be black or red, Palestinian or Jew, male or female, fight to establish their identity, it is crucial that we males, too, try to define ourselves and explain, if only to each other, what it means to be a man. A map of Seneca Falls in its greatest historical context helps me explore and understand what it means to be a white man at this point at the beginning of a new millennium.

If white men like me can understand the mythic implications of what happened in Seneca Falls, and redraw our personal maps accordingly, there is hope that we will not have to crash and burn in an apocalyptic confrontation with women and people of color. White males have already lost the exclusive rights to the reins of civilization. It happened in Seneca Falls. It may not seem obvious, but the psychic underpinnings of white male manifest destiny were loosened and melted there in the fires of change when Elizabeth Cady Stanton demanded the vote.

What remained after this psychic shift? In one sense, all American men, and most men of the modern world, whether they know it or not, are men from Seneca Falls. That is, modern men are the products of the fierce and ongoing feminism that blazed forth in Seneca Falls. Although the Seneca Falls Convention was only a moment in a continuing women's movement, as a result of its two-day proceedings in the now defunct Wesleyan Chapel, women were changed politically and intellectually. Because of this men would have to change too, forever. We are still in that process.

For much of United States history, men were granted power, authority, and supremacy by virtue of simply being

male. In the eyes of the law, they were primary. In being educated, they were favored. In the hierarchy of the church, they
were unquestionably superior, and in the market place, they
were paid more. And, of course, if men are granted primary
importance in significant contexts, then they begin to act
importantly. Perhaps they even become inured to the fact that
their sense of self-worth is built, however consciously or
unconsciously, on the subordination of women. In the case of
Southern, slave-holding society, white male authority rested
on the subjugation of black people as well.

Given this prevailing culture, for Elizabeth Cady Stanton
to refuse to be subordinated was a revolutionary, heroic act.
Her courage would not only open the polling booth to
women, but would also help ignite the feminist transformation of American women.

It was not surprising that after living in a social order that
put white men on top and women and black slaves on the
bottom, white men were reluctant to give way. In addition
to the political havoc women's equality would certainly
wreak, men perceived that its effects on their personal relationships would necessarily be disturbing, if not devastating.
If men base their lives on the assumption that women will
only affirm and support them, and if that affirming, support-
ive role ceases, then at least temporarily, men will be disoriented, angry, and lost.

As a man from Seneca Falls I have a unique opportunity
to examine my relationship to womankind and particularly
to Elizabeth Cady Stanton, especially if I also meet Frederick Douglass face to face in the soul-town of Seneca Falls.
The enslavement of black people for more than two hundred
years prior to the Civil War is perhaps even more obviously
repugnant than the legal and religious hegemony of males
over females. So while it is vital to me to return to Seneca
Falls in order to discover a knowing relationship with women
at the deepest levels, it becomes equally important, almost
coincidentally so, that I look into the face of Frederick Douglass as well. He was a black man in a country in which black

men, women, and children were sold as though they were animals, a country that even now has immense difficulty in perceiving, let alone resolving, the political and social issues that haunt our multiracial society. And, man from Seneca Falls that I am, I cannot study his words, or even look at his face, without facing my own fears about and my relationship to the black man.

The relationship between white society and black people during slavery was well defined. The laws that protected slavery, the economic conditions that encouraged it, the racist customs and taboos that tended to manage and perpetuate it, clearly specified the appropriate attitude of white to black, which was master to slave, superior to inferior. Frederick Douglass's antislavery and women's rights work challenges at the root a civilization so infected. And I inherit the legacy of his work, his charge to all Americans to break the chains between master and slave.

For the white American male, long accustomed to having ascendancy over the female sex and the black race, the Seneca Falls Convention was an economic and political defeat. But, luckily, within the very terms of this radical moment, the white male was also given the means of his healing. Elizabeth Cady Stanton and Frederick Douglass, genuine examples of Joseph Campbell's definition of the classic hero, carry the power to heal and transform the white American man who pays attention to the true history of Seneca Falls. It is that history I circumambulate, hoping that my own male charge will be ionized in the spirit of a new world which the events of Seneca Falls, in part, inaugurate.

I take pains here to get the story straight, to describe accurately the Woman's Rights Convention and Elizabeth Cady Stanton's and Frederick Douglass's presence there. But I also understand the events of Seneca Falls as a Jungian psychoanalyst might understand a dream — in this case a distinctly American dream. These two potent figures literally forced their way in among the rigid hierarchies of their time, revolutionizing everything. By taking their rightful places in the political and social American community, they made true democracy at least theoretically possible for the first time.

White men today are still vibrating from the intensity of those heroic acts, still casting about for the foothold lost when their privilege was undone. Particularly because I grew up in Seneca Falls, the dream of the Seneca Falls Convention is my personal dream. It has been disturbing my sleep ever since I became aware as a teenager of what happened on the downtown streets of my home town. My seventh-grade social studies teacher was the first to alert me to the convention, but did so exclusively in regard to Elizabeth Cady Stanton. Indeed, most scholarly treatments of the Seneca Falls Convention make only passing reference to the vital role played by Frederick Douglass. If I can get to the bottom of what it means to be a man from Seneca Falls, and hence from America itself, I think I might be made whole, rendered somehow in tune with the promise of American democracy.

Seneca Falls was not only located on the "psychic highway" of the reform movements of abolition, temperance, millennialism, and women's rights; it was also an industrial mecca. Almost overnight, mills and factories mushroomed along the Seneca River. So in addition to discovering an initiation into manhood that would honor the equality of women and African Americans, I cannot escape confronting the hard-bitten rational mind that values the machine and industrial strength above all else, which Western civilization has come to represent.

In Seneca Falls, then, I have at my doorstep the conflicting contemporary forces that are rapidly and lethally converging upon us. These demand our recognition and reconciliation or else will cause our destruction. As a man from Seneca Falls, I must find the way out of (or is it the way into?) the modern maze of feminism, social equality, and intoxicating, often toxic, technology (which some feminists even call "patriarchal technology"). The goal is to slay those minotaur aspects of the white male that cannot be carried alive into the next century, and to find and celebrate the long-overdue transformation of his essential self.

In taking this journey, we will be returning to a kind of zero-point of consciousness, to the Seneca Falls that was once known as Shaseonce by the people indigenous to the place. If white American males can arrive at a prehistoric point of original soul, then we might be inclined to begin again, this time tutored by heroes, fit for a new age, spiritualized perhaps for the first time in centuries. The way to Seneca Falls lies along the path of a diverse humanity that constitutes this nation, and arrives in a sacred city to which I, and all Americans, belong.

CHAPTER TWO

Locating Seneca Falls

Like slavery, the prevailing, church-blessed tradition of American women as second-class citizens was paradoxical for a young nation born out of revolution. Women were not allowed to vote. They could not will property or continue to own property they brought into a marriage or earned while being married, although the groundbreaking 1848 Married Woman's Property Act of New York State granted married women the right to hold title to property independent of their husbands. Even with this historic law, however, women in New York and in most states could not buy or sell without their husbands' consent, were not given custody of their children when circumstances required the dissolution of a marriage, and did not inherit equally with their children upon the death of their spouse. Their lack of civil, religious, and intellectual freedom was, in the eyes of Elizabeth Cady Stanton, a form of human bondage.

Until the Seneca Falls Convention, and for some time afterward, most American women's political activities were confined to the causes of antislavery and temperance. Many of these were undertaken within the context of "religious benevolence," the term for fundraising and volunteer work for the destitute and "the heathen," including the unredeemed who lived overseas. Women were active and outspoken, but only from behind the veil of a demure, nonpolitical stance. They were essentially cheerleaders, lobbying and supporting movements that were actually led and inspired by male religious leaders, political activists, and politicians. The abolitionist movement, however, provided women with a context for addressing individual, God-given rights to freedom and self-determination, not only for those in slavery, but eventually for women themselves. To demand the vote for women, as Elizabeth Cady Stanton did, was to demand that women become political players to be reckoned with, and even feared.

Elizabeth Cady Stanton's husband, Henry, was himself an active reformer, abolitionist, and political worker. Although he generally supported his wife's activism, he threatened to leave town during the convention if she included the demand for the vote along with the other resolutions (see Appendix 2) she was attaching to the convention's Declaration of Rights and Sentiments. She did and he did.

When one of Elizabeth Cady Stanton's sisters, Harriet, also signed the declaration, their father immediately went to Seneca Falls to urge his daughters to retract their signatures. Harriet did so, Elizabeth did not (Banner, 47).

Given their political and social subordination, women had already achieved skill and a certain power as influential consultants to their husbands. In fact, this power of artful persuasion from behind the demure veil of marriage was in large measure responsible for the fierce opposition of some women to the cause of women's rights. By going public as women's rights proponents, many believed that their already scant power might be further diminished. This explains why some women who were just becoming active in the movement for women's rights refused at the time to sign the Declaration of Rights and Sentiments.

Born November 12, 1815, in Johnstown, New York, Elizabeth Cady grew up hearing the omnipresent, Pavlovian ringing of the church bells that announced school, church, prayer meetings, funerals, and so forth (Banner, 3). From the time she first overheard desperate women seeking legal help from her father, the local attorney and judge, through the harsh circumstances of trying to raise a large family almost single-handedly in dreary Seneca Falls, to her emergence as the "foremother" philosopher, writer, speaker, and visionary of the women's rights movement, Elizabeth spoke up, acted, and strived for women's equality.

As a youngster in Johnstown, she had heard male visitors commiserating with her parents that Katherine, her newly born younger sister, was unfortunately just another girl. When Elizabeth Cady came of age, women still were not admitted to college, and after graduating from the Troy Female Seminary in 1833, she did what most other young unmarried women from well-to-do families did at the time: she engaged in charitable activities associated with her family's church. One of her projects was to raise money for an aspiring minister to attend seminary, a task she and other women successfully accomplished. When he came back to town he preached in his benefactors' presence a sermon on the inferiority of women. In what must have been a stunning act, Elizabeth and some of her fellow fundraisers stood up and walked out of the church.

To put in perspective the degree of the social and educational restraints inherent in society during Stanton's time, consider that the first female physician in America graduated from the Geneva Medical College in Geneva, New York, only in 1848. Not until 1869 would a woman be licensed to practice law in the United States. Predictably, then, the press's reaction to the Seneca Falls Woman's Rights Convention was vitriolic. The writers of the day characterized such activist women as Amazons, frustrated spinsters, and a threat to the unity and decorum of the institution of marriage, the family, and the entire social order of the nation (Banner, 46).

Women's fashions were based on petticoats, long skirts, frills, and corsets, duly reflecting their wearers' social and political constraints. Elizabeth Cady Stanton's cousin Elizabeth Smith Miller, visiting in Seneca Falls in 1850, wore a costume of her own design, consisting of comfortable baggy trousers and a short dress. The garb, publicized in Amelia Bloomer's temperance newsletter, *The Lily*, and soon worn by Elizabeth Cady Stanton, Amelia Bloomer, and other activist women, came to be known as "bloomers." Public reaction to this "mannish" dress was overwhelmingly negative; the bloomers were attacked as an assault on marriage and family, and a threat to everything that was traditional and decent.

One writer of the time, Grace Greenwood, described Stanton as having "a comfortable look of motherliness and a sly benignancy in her smiling eyes, even though her arguments have been bayonet thrusts and her words gun shots" (quoted in Banner, 123). This is a particularly violent image to describe a woman raised to be a model of female decorum in an age of strictly defined sex roles. Certainly neither Stanton nor any of her female colleagues advocated violence. But clearly her writing and speaking were so powerful that they were considered forceful enough to rip and tear, if not destroy, the country's social, religious, and legal fabric.

The inequality of women was so pervasive in every institution, every custom, and most social assumptions of the time, that it was invisible. We should not doubt the tenacity and strength of character necessary for the tasks Elizabeth Cady Stanton and her coworkers undertook for decades in the name of reform and the rights of women.

According to Stanton, the "aristocracy of sex" went back centuries upon centuries, to before the origins of Judaism and Christianity, back to the time when a more benevolent matriarchy was usurped by an emerging patriarchy, with its brute power and superior weapons. It was this almost seamless hegemony of male dominance that was called into question in Seneca Falls in 1848. And the quiet, eloquent voice of Elizabeth Cady Stanton was heard round the world:

> I should feel exceedingly diffident to appear before you at this time, having never before spoken in public, were I not nerved by a sense of right and duty, did I not feel that the time had come for the question of woman's wrongs to be laid before the public, did I not believe that woman herself must do this work; for woman alone can understand the height, the depth, the length of her degradation. (*Correspondence, Writings, Speeches*, 28)

Stanton earned her heroic aspect as one who presides over the dismemberment and symbolic regeneration of a society. In place of the old order she was eviscerating with her Declaration of Sentiments and various other resolutions, she would go on to create, define, shape, and bless, in her writings and her speeches, the spiritual blueprint of a new civilization based on sexual equality.

Stanton put her radical roots down deep in the isolated and rustic town of Seneca Falls, with its booming industrial economy and its muddy streets. She would become a zealous abolitionist, a social thinker, an advocate for more liberal divorce laws, a proponent of birth control, a supporter of co-education, a critic of Christianity, the first woman to run for the Congress of the United States, an opponent of abortion, a regular on the lyceum, or speaking tour, and always she would persist as a clarion voice and political force for women's suffrage.

While living in Seneca Falls from 1847 to 1862, Stanton entertained and consulted with many of the other important reformers of the time, as they passed through that part of upstate New York known as the "reform belt" and along the Western Turnpike, the main east/west thoroughfare of the region. She became progressively clearer and more radical in her perception that women individually had to plumb the depths of their own independent intellectual and spiritual selves before they could truly effect the vital self-empowerment and self-realization of their sex.

She met Susan B. Anthony in Seneca Falls in 1851, when Anthony came to attend one of William Lloyd Garrison's antislavery rallies. Anthony's gritty organizing and research coupled with the philosophic vision and grand conceptual designs of Elizabeth Cady Stanton succeeded in influencing millions of women to begin a process of serious self-examination and political activism.

Stanton had lobbied for the New York State Married Woman's Property Act. When first introduced in 1836, the bill failed to attract enough votes for adoption. Following an economic panic in 1837, the bill was resurrected when wealthy men became aware of the risk of losing their wives' property to their own creditors. "Fathers like Judge Cady, whose entire fortune would be inherited by married daughters, also had an interest in guaranteeing its safekeeping from errant sons-in-law. At first more men than women expressed an interest in the issue." The bill gained momentum, and while Elizabeth Cady Stanton lived in Albany during the early 1840s, she circulated petitions on its behalf and lobbied members of the legislature. It passed finally in April 1848, was amended once in 1857, and another bill, which enlarged its scope, was passed in 1860 with the help of Stanton, Susan B. Anthony, and their colleagues (Griffith, 43, 100).

By the spring of 1852, Stanton, with a little politicking help from Anthony, became president of the New York State Woman's Temperance Society. Other members included women's rights workers Lucy Stone, Ernestine Rose, as well as Lucretia Mott and Martha Wright who helped organize the Seneca Falls Convention. Stanton delivered her acceptance address wearing bloomers and sounded the themes that would animate her work for the rest of her life. Most of her audience were still working in the tradition of activism through religious benevolence. To this arm of the incipient women's movement, she "declared that the ending of poverty and the oppression of women was more important than sending missionaries and bibles to the heathen; to temperance compatriots she stressed the need for divorce for chronic drunkenness. Yet she also declared her intention to address social ills involved in marriage, prostitution, and the general subjection of women and called on her audience to end their dependency on men and their general 'lethargy, the shackles of a false education, customs, and habits'" (Banner, 62).

Throughout the 1850s and 1860s, Stanton and Susan B. Anthony together fought the battles for suffrage, divorce reform, and the rights of working women. Stanton opposed male membership in the temperance organization of which she was president, but was outvoted. Although she was ousted a year later by a coalition of men and conservative women, the fight for women's rights had gained a momentum that could no longer be stemmed.

In 1862 Stanton moved with her family to New York City, where her husband had secured a position in the New York City Customs House, and where two of her sisters already resided. By then, New York was a much more culturally sophisticated reform stage than Seneca Falls. Nevertheless, Seneca Falls remains a sacred city of the feminist movement, the birthplace of a myth that would initiate a fundamental change in the relationship between men and women.

CHAPTER THREE

✥

The Seneca Falls Convention

The Stantons moved to Seneca Falls in 1847, putting them near the strong reform activity thriving in Rochester and Buffalo in the heart of the reform belt stretching from Ohio through Pennsylvania, upstate New York, and into western Massachusetts and Boston. Martha Wright, the sister of Lucretia Mott who already had earned a strong reputation as a reformer and women's rights advocate, lived in nearby Auburn, where the reform governor and antislavery politician William Henry Seward also lived. In Waterloo, three miles west of Seneca Falls, there was a community of reform-minded Quakers known as Hicksites.

Situated at the northern tip of Cayuga Lake, on the Seneca River, and roughly equidistant from Rochester and Syracuse, Seneca Falls was a heavily industrialized town of about 3,000 people. Its muddy streets and its distance from a metropolitan center almost gave it the feel of a frontier town. The Stanton house on Washington Street was about a mile from the center of town on unpaved streets. The Stantons already had three children — they would have seven in all — and all three were often sick with respiratory ailments. It was said that the house was always in an uproar. With a husband frequently away on business and political work, Elizabeth Stanton felt painfully isolated, and experienced, despite her class background, the essence of what it meant to be a wife and mother, tied down to the drudgery of running a household, cut off from other adults and from intellectual culture, and without precious minutes in the day to sit down to think or write. Having been close to the heartbeat of reform activity in association with her cousin Gerrit Smith, having tasted the fire of exclusion as a woman from the proceedings at the World Anti-Slavery Convention in London in 1840, and sharing only intermittent intellectual camaraderie with her fellow reformers in Boston, Elizabeth Cady Stanton felt politically and personally isolated in Seneca Falls.

The Seneca Falls Convention lasted only two days, July 19 and 20, 1848. A rather spontaneous meeting preceded it by six days, held at the Waterloo home of Jane Hunt. In addition to Stanton and Hunt, this planning meeting was attended by Lucretia Mott and Mary Ann McClintock, both Hicksites, and Martha Wright. The Hicksites were already active, within the charter of their religion, in women's rights issues. At the meeting, Stanton was particularly vehement and eloquent on the subject of women's oppression. Her feelings of personal exasperation sparked a diatribe against the privileges of men and the current political and social circumstances of American women. She talked passionately about the injustices inherent in society at large, and proposed a convention to discuss these matters publicly. "The question of equal rights among the Hicksites predisposed them to be responsive to Stanton's outburst." Mott and McClintock had just returned a week earlier from the Hicksites' annual meeting in which they had deliberated on the question of "how to minister to the Indian remnants in upstate New York" (Griffith, 52).

The group decided to convene a meeting on the rights of women. Use of the Wesleyan Chapel was secured that same day, and an announcement was placed in the *Seneca County Courier* that ran the next (Griffith, 52). The announcement read:

> Woman's Rights Convention — A convention to discuss the social, civil, and religious rights of woman will be held in the Wesleyan Chapel, Seneca Falls, New York, on Wednesday and Thursday, the 19th and 20th of July, current; commencing at ten o'clock a.m. During the first day, the meeting will be held exclusively for women who are earnestly invited to attend. The public are generally invited to be present on the second day,

when Lucretia Mott of Philadelphia, and other ladies and gentlemen will address the meeting. (Seneca Falls Historical Society, *Debut*, 11)

The group decided to meet the following Sunday "to set the agenda, draft a document for discussion and some resolutions, and decide on subjects for speeches." Referring to that second meeting of July 16, also held in Waterloo, Stanton's biographer, Elisabeth Griffith, tells us: "When the women gathered around Mary Ann McClintock's parlor table, they did not know how to begin. As Stanton recalled their dilemma in the *History*, 'they felt as helpless and hopeless as if they had been suddenly asked to construct a steam engine'" (quoted in Griffith, 52).[1]

The women worked collaboratively at this meeting to itemize the various grievances women commonly felt toward men. They examined "various masculine productions . . . but all alike seemed too tame and pacific for the inauguration of a rebellion" (Stanton quoted in Griffith, 53). Stanton proposed that they use the Declaration of Independence as the model document by which to present their grievances, substituting "all men" for the tyrant King George, and it was she who prepared it (Griffith, 53). They named it "A Declaration of Rights and Sentiments."

Lucretia Mott especially wanted women's economic and social injustices to be addressed at the convention. Elizabeth Cady Stanton saw the right to vote as the fulcrum for a revolution in all spheres, using a logic based on the eighteenth-century doctrine of natural rights, which she, "like the abolitionists . . . applied to nineteenth-century sexual inequality" (Griffith, 54).

According to Griffith,

The wife, daughter, and cousin of politicians and lawyers, she

---

[1] *History* is a reference to *The History of Woman's Suffrage*, a multi-volume work completed by Elizabeth Cady Stanton, Susan B. Anthony, Matilda Joslyn Gage, and Ida Husted Harper. The first volume appeared in 1881.

was convinced that social problems required political solutions. Like the political abolitionists with whom she was allied, Elizabeth Cady Stanton believed in using government to create legal remedies. Since women without voting rights had no independent access to political power, she advocated suffrage. The combination of Mott's economic concerns and Stanton's political instincts made the Declaration a comprehensive document. (54)

On July 19, at ten o'clock, when Stanton and her colleagues tried to enter the chapel, they discovered that it was locked. Stanton had her nephew crawl through a window and unlock the door, and so the proceedings began. Close to three hundred interested people attended the convention. Of these, about thirty were men, including Frederick Douglass, the eloquent editor of the *North Star,* the abolitionist newspaper published in Rochester. In attendance, too, were many other committed reformers, as well as some aggrieved female factory workers from the local Seneca Falls mills. Among these was young Charlotte Woodward, a glove factory worker from Seneca Falls, who signed the declaration and would be the only woman present at the convention to live to cast a vote following the passage in 1920 of the Nineteenth Amendment to the U. S. Constitution.

Wednesday, the first day of the convention, was devoted to the reading and discussion of the Declaration of Rights and Sentiments (see Appendix 1 for text) and its fifteen grievances; the presentation of eleven related resolutions, including the ninth, which demanded the right to vote for women; and speeches by Stanton and other women's rights advocates. Years later, Stanton recalled that when she took the podium on that first day she felt like "suddenly abandoning all her principles and running away." Amelia Bloomer said that Stanton spoke so softly that it was impossible to hear her (Banner, 41–42). That evening Lucretia Mott spoke on the progress of the reform movement.

The second day was given to more discussion and to voting on the resolutions attached to the declaration. (The complete resolutions presented to the convention can be found in Appendix 2.) While all the other resolutions were passed unanimously, the one calling for the vote for women passed by a bare majority. Frederick Douglass spoke strongly in its favor, the only man to do so.

The Declaration of Sentiments set forth grievances to be addressed, provided a mission statement for the full social, religious, and political emancipation of women, and demanded that women have "immediate admission to all the rights and privileges which belong to them as citizens of the United States" (*Debut*, 13).

According to one historian, the declaration

> set forth the unjust subjection of women, and man's usurpa-
> tion of her rights, stating that he had never allowed her to exer-
> cise her right to vote; that she was compelled to submit to laws
> which she could not formulate; and it pointed out that the sin-
> gle women were taxed to support a government which did not
> recognize them except for this financial support; that man had
> refused to let women pursue profitable occupations, or to
> receive a thorough education, and allowed only a subordinate
> position in church, thus trying in every way to minimize her
> self-respect and destroy her confidence in her own strength and
> ability. (*Debut*, 13)

Stanton herself was the author of Resolution Number Nine, calling for women's right to vote: "RESOLVED, That it is the duty of the women of this country to secure to them- selves their sacred right to the elective franchise." The Quak- ers at the meeting voted against the resolution because, as pacifists, they would turn away from any proposed voting in national elections, as it might be pursuant to war.

Stanton's own speech to the Seneca Falls Convention, delivered that Wednesday, July 19, 1848, powerfully sets forth the agenda of the emerging women's struggle with clar- ity and wit. (A fuller version is contained in Appendix 3.)

> We have met here today to discuss our rights and wrongs, civil
> and political, and not, as some have supposed, to go into the

detail of social life alone. We do not propose to petition the legislature to make our husbands just, generous and courteous, to seat every man at the head of a cradle, and to clothe every woman in male attire. . . .

We are assembled to protest against a form of government, existing without the consent of the governed — to declare our right to be free as man is free, to be represented in the government which we are taxed to support, to have such disgraceful laws as give man the power to chastise and imprison his wife, to take the wages which she earns, the property which she inherits, and, in the case of separation, the children of her love; laws which make her the mere dependent on his bounty. It is to protest against such unjust laws as these that we are assembled today, and to have them, if possible, forever erased from our statute-books, deeming them a shame and a disgrace to a Christian republic in the nineteenth century. . . .

. . . To have drunkards, idiots, horse-racing, rumselling rowdies, ignorant foreigners, and silly boys fully recognized, while we ourselves are thrust out from all the rights that belong to citizens, it is too grossly insulting to the dignity of woman to be longer quietly submitted to. The right is ours. Have it we must. Use it we will. The pens, the tongues, the fortunes, the indomitable wills of many women are already pledged to secure this right. The great truth, that no just government can be formed without the consent of the governed, we shall echo and re-echo in the ears of the unjust judge until by continual coming we shall weary him. . . .

. . . Verily, the world waits the coming of some new element, some purifying power, some spirit of mercy and love. The voice of woman has been silenced in the state, the church, and the home, but man cannot fulfill his destiny alone, he cannot redeem his race unaided. . . . The world has never seen a truly great and virtuous nation, because in the degradation of woman the very fountains of life are poisoned at their source. It is vain to look for silver and gold from mines of copper and lead. It is the wise mother that has the wise son. So long as your women are slaves you may throw your colleges and churches to the winds. . . . Truly are the sins of the fathers visited upon the children to the third and fourth generation. God, in his wisdom, has so linked the whole human family together that any violence done at one end of the chain is felt throughout its length, and here, too, is the law of restoration, as in woman all have fallen, so in her elevation shall the race be recreated.

. . . We do not expect our path to be strewn with flowers of popular applause. . . . (*Correspondence, Writings, Speeches*, 28–35)

In the years following the convention, Stanton's increasingly radical pronouncements culminated with her feminist analysis of the Bible and her participation in a remarkable international council of women. If a tolerable new era was to be born, she insisted, women would have to achieve an active voice in culture, politics, and religion (Donovan, 39). She characterized the reluctant citizenry and the ranks of the married "a multitude of timid, underdeveloped men and women, afraid of priests and politicians" (quoted in Banner, 64). Her pronouncements were so stinging that well into the twentieth century antisuffrage forces continued to smart at what they saw as her heretical antichurch, prolabor, antifamily stance (Griffith, xv).

Because of the hackles she raised even within the women's rights movement, Stanton would be relegated to the back rooms of feminist activity in the last years of her life by younger suffragists who celebrated the work of Susan B. Anthony (Griffith, xv). But by calling for women's right to vote, Elizabeth Cady Stanton struck at the very heart of the oppression of women, making the women's movement from that point on inexorably political, no longer able to fit neatly under the banner of religious tradition. Other regional women's rights conventions and a national convention held in Worcester, Massachusetts, in 1850, followed on the heels of the Seneca Falls Convention. At most of these, the Seneca Falls Declaration of Rights and Sentiments was read and discussed. Stanton's women's rights activities, coupled with her work in the antislavery movement, would advance the process of peeling back the complex layers of social, legal, and religious oppression in America to reveal the human beings at the center: men and women, black and white.

CHAPTER FOUR

Mother Stanton

Even Elizabeth Cady Stanton's physiognomy provides clues for men's homecoming. Her face is plain and round, like a roll of cotton fabric. In photographs, she looks right at the camera, nailing you with her stare. There are no frills, no forced smiles, nothing to distract from her basic personhood.

From a man's point of view, her appeal may not be sexual, although we know she enjoyed her sexuality and said so publicly at a time when to do so was considered outrageous. Her face as a young woman has much youthful sensuality that seems to weave itself into the long, languishing curls and the direct "I dare you" look.

Her hair was white during her mature years and she became truly obese toward the end of her life, weighing about 250 pounds. Her face remained smooth, round, somehow complete, with the expression of a no-nonsense, mature woman who never for a moment doubted the full panoply of her powers. She offers a totally credible look of competence and maturity and of impending, right-minded action. Thus, in her appearance, Elizabeth Cady Stanton stands guardian at the door of female power. Cloaked in a black silk dress, she rose up in Seneca Falls as though from the dark unconsciousness to which men assigned women and members of minority groups, to proclaim the fact of women's personhood.

In the 1820s, when Elizabeth Cady was still just a girl, Flora Campbell came to consult Elizabeth's father, near Albany, New York. Flora Campbell had been a servant of the Cady family and continued to provide them with farm produce after she had left their employ. Flora asked Judge Cady how she might recover the farm that she and her husband had purchased with their joint funds, for her now-deceased husband had summarily willed it to her wastrel son. As the young Elizabeth listened, her father explained to Flora that legally nothing could be done to recover the farm because the law considered a woman's possessions the property of her husband. Married women were not much more than extensions of their husbands in the eyes of the law, which gave husbands complete rights over their wives' property, earnings, and children. Wives were not even permitted to testify against their husbands (Banner, 8).

Upon hearing what her father said, Elizabeth decided to cut the offending laws out of her father's law books with a knife and, some days later, actually attempted to do so. Discovering her in the act, Judge Cady is said to have explained to his daughter that laws do not live merely in law books. According to Stanton's reminiscences, her father went on to suggest that she might work to change such laws when she grew up. This moment left a burning imprint on her soul.

Stanton took much pride in her lineage, which descended on her mother's side from the local Livingston clan. An immediate Livingston forebear had been an officer in the Colonial army of the Revolutionary War. As a mature thinker, she would consider herself to be a daughter of the revolution in a literal and intellectual sense, one who was continuing the work of giving birth to the ideals of this relatively young democracy.

The Cady family had a black servant, a man named Peter Teabout, who looked after the children and whom Elizabeth loved dearly. Teabout would take the girls on adventures to the local courthouse and jail. Later, Stanton would attribute her interest in the law and in prison reform partly to these visits, and her witness of the prejudice expressed toward Teabout predisposed her toward her later abolitionist work (Banner, 6).

The Cady children were frequent visitors at the residence of their cousin Gerrit Smith in Peterboro, New York, outside

Syracuse. Both Smith and his wife, Ann Fitzhugh, were liberal and outspoken on the controversial subjects of the day, and their home was a gathering place for many of the leaders and opinion setters on the reform lecture circuit.

Smith became disillusioned early on with the church-centered efforts to give to the poor, convert the unredeemed, and raise funds for overseas missionary work. By 1830 his primary interest had become temperance, and by 1835 he was an abolitionist. In this progression, he was typical of the reformers of the pre–Civil War era, who moved from a cloistered religious perspective to a political, more worldly one (Banner, 17). Through this process, Smith's home became a station on the Underground Railroad.

It was at the Smith residence that Elizabeth Cady met Henry Brewster Stanton. Ten years older than she and then an executive of the American Anti-Slavery Society, Stanton was also an occasional newspaper reporter. Later, in August 1848, just weeks after the Seneca Falls Convention, Henry Stanton and other abolitionists formed the Free-Soil Party. Eventually he would become active in the newly emerging Republican Party.

Elizabeth and Henry were married in 1840 in a ceremony that omitted the woman's standard promise "to obey." She explained in later years that she deliberately retained her maiden name, making the analogy to what she observed to be the first meaningful act of freed slaves, that of taking a full, real name. The couple traveled to New Jersey to visit Henry's friends Theodore Dwight Weld and his wife, Angelina Grimke Weld, his associates in the antislavery movement. Angelina's sister, Sarah, was also a known abolitionist. For their wedding trip, Henry and Elizabeth traveled to the World Anti-Slavery Convention in London that year.

Founded in 1833, the American Anti-Slavery Society had split in 1839 over the issue of whether or not to allow women to participate in its proceedings. This issue was carried across the Atlantic by Elizabeth Cady Stanton and her husband and all the other United States delegates on their way to the

World Anti-Slavery Convention. Through her politicizing experiences at Gerrit Smith's and her association with her husband's abolitionist colleagues, Elizabeth was well acquainted with William Lloyd Garrison, the fiery abolitionist speaker and publicist. The New York contingent, of which Henry Stanton was a delegate, wanted women excluded. But the Boston and Philadelphia supporters of Garrison succeeded in allowing women to be seated, but apart and behind a screen.

All the Garrison contingent stayed in the same boarding house in a section of London called Cheapside. Rather than remain with the New York group, Henry chose to be with his wife there. At dinner at their boarding house, Elizabeth Cady Stanton met the renowned American Quaker activist, Lucretia Mott, who was already active in reform politics in the United States. At table, Mott spoke vehemently in favor of women's participation in the Anti-Slavery Convention.

Elizabeth Cady Stanton witnessed Mott preach a sermon in a London Unitarian church to a sexually mixed audience, a rare event at the time. While in London, Stanton first proposed to Mott that they hold a women's rights convention when they returned to the States. Eight formative years would elapse before it would actually be planned and executed, but Stanton's reform-mindedness had been awakened.

During the Civil War, women's rights work slowed. Women in Northern states eagerly supported the cause of the Union army by fundraising and by filling government jobs left vacant by men who had gone to war. Women activists generally honored abolitionist appeals to suspend women's rights work until the war was won and slavery abolished. Conservative women even successfully scaled back earlier feminist victories. For example, in 1862 New York rescinded much of the ground-breaking 1860 Married Woman's Property Act (Banner, 91).

Between 1863 and 1869, Elizabeth Cady Stanton and Susan B. Anthony worked feverishly to regain the momentum for women's rights that had been building prior to the war, while they also supported efforts to gain rights for the freed slaves of the South. In 1863, they organized the Woman's Loyal National League, essentially a petition campaign to demand that Congress emancipate all Southern slaves. The resolutions passed at the organizational meeting included the demand for the full emancipation of women at the war's end. By 1864, Stanton, Anthony, and their coworkers had collected 400,000 signatures in favor of the Thirteenth Amendment, the largest such campaign ever (Griffith, 112). Senator Charles Sumner of Massachusetts presented the signatures to the United States Senate. In January of the next year, Congress passed the Thirteenth Amendment, abolishing slavery.

In 1866, in New York City, Elizabeth Cady Stanton became the first woman to run as a candidate for the House of Representatives, taking advantage of the fact that although women could not vote, they were not legally barred from running for office. But the decision to run was a hasty one, and the campaign was largely unrealized. Of the 20,000 votes counted, Stanton received twenty-four (Banner, 93).

In a move that was reminiscent of the difficulties of trying to merge the women's rights and abolitionist movements prior to the war, Elizabeth Cady Stanton and Susan B. Anthony tried in 1866 to forge the National Woman's Rights Convention, which had suspended its annual meetings in 1860, into a coalition advocating for the rights of women and blacks. The majority of delegates feared that by linking the two issues in the public mind, both would die. Most contended that this critical moment in American history belonged to the struggle for black liberation, and that it was vital to keep public attention focused there.

The period of Reconstruction following the Civil War gained its name from U.S. government efforts to rebuild and reorganize Southern life and to put blacks on equal footing with whites. Elizabeth Cady Stanton saw Reconstruction as the opportunity to effect a second revolution in America, one in which the whole society — its churches, its schools, its families, and its governments — could be cleansed of their class, race, and gender inequalities and by which a true republic could be achieved.

By moderating her views on women's suffrage during and after the war, Stanton thought she might gain political allies to help make women's suffrage part of any legislative package granting citizenship to the freed slaves. She was bitterly disappointed when the Fourteenth and Fifteenth Amendments, granting black males citizenship and voting rights, excluded women.

The team of Stanton and Anthony petitioned both presidential nomination conventions in 1868 to include suffrage planks. Neither party acquiesced. Transferring their lobbying efforts permanently from New York to Washington, they founded the National Woman Suffrage Association in 1869. The goal was a Sixteenth Amendment to the U. S. Constitution that would give women the right to vote. And, in March 1869, allies in Congress introduced such an amendment, but it would be fifty years before the goal was realized. Later that same year, Lucy Stone and Antoinette Brown Blackwell organized the rival American Woman Suffrage Association.

Disappointed and frustrated that the feminist agenda was being overshadowed by black issues, Stanton made remarks that demeaned the ex-slave population, fulminating that while suffrage was not legal for American women, it was to be granted to ignorant black men. While many of her apparently racist and xenophobic remarks can be understood as rhetoric designed to keep the women's rights agenda front and center, "it is also true that America's foremost feminist held paternalistic views about blacks, immigrants, workers, and Cubans" (Griffith, 206). Late in her career, Stanton promoted suffrage for the educated classes only, making her vulnerable to charges of elitism. But for Stanton, education was the best guard against prejudice of any kind and was therefore the foundation of a true democracy.

The National Woman Suffrage Association and the American Woman Suffrage Association merged in 1890, with

Elizabeth Cady Stanton as its president and a broad range of social and political resolutions as its agenda. From its first meeting emerged an International Council of Women, with a domestic U.S. branch, the National Council of Women. Stanton delivered both the opening and closing remarks at this unifying meeting, speaking in favor of a global women's movement.

She observed, "In every country, we see the wisest statesmen at their wits' end vainly trying to meet the puzzling questions of the hour: in Russia, it is nihilism; in Germany, socialism; in France, communism; in England, home rule for Ireland . . . and in America, land, labor, taxes, tariffs, temperance and woman suffrage. Where shall we look for the new power whereby the race can be lifted up?" (quoted in Banner, 152). For her, it was women who possessed such power.

Elizabeth Cady Stanton resigned the presidency of the merged National American Woman Suffrage Association after two years, on the occasion of her address on "The Solitude of Self." After that she never attended another NAWSA meeting. This speech effectively expressed her philosophy embracing a process of individual self-realization that she saw as crucial to men as well as to women, a philosophy essentially differing from the thought of the next generational wave of suffragists. (See Appendix 4.)

According to the feminist scholar Ellen Carol DuBois, editor of Stanton's writings:

[Stanton's] basic message was "the infinite diversity in human character" and the necessity of equal rights for all individuals, themes which had always been central to her feminism. Her approach to women's emancipation, which stressed the liberation of each woman's unique capacities and inclinations, was being eclipsed by an emphasis on that which was allegedly common to all women, the attributes and qualities that women, once freed of male influence, were expected to share. Stanton conceded the claims of gender, the fact that women had common concerns as "mother, wife, sister, and daughter," and even more as a sex equal in importance to men. However, in determining women's rights, both of these considerations were far less important to her than 'the individuality of each human soul,' the human condition which simultaneously distinguishes each of us from the other, and is common to us all, women and men alike. . . . The new note Stanton struck as she insisted on the 'solitude of self' was existential. Although she urged women to continue to fight for equality in the 'outer conditions of human beings,' she also encouraged them to struggle for full development and independence in the 'inner' aspects as well. . . . Her bequest to the women of the future stressed the psychological dimension of freedom and defended the importance of individual self-determination for women. (187–88).

In 1888, Stanton wrote: "Society is based on this four-fold bondage of woman — Church, State, Capital and Society, making liberty and equality for her antagonistic to every organized institution" (quoted in Banner, 145). Of these, she believed, the limitations posed by traditional Christianity were particularly inhibiting to the full development of women. "False theology," as she called it, represented the final stumbling block before the solitude of self could be achieved in an ultimate sense. Stanton attempted to gain the support of the National Woman Suffrage Association in a campaign against Christianity as it had come to be expressed, but failed.

Over the final decades of her life, traditional religion's constraint of women, and its admonition that they assume silence in church, occupied much of her serious thought, culminating in *The Woman's Bible,* published in 1895. *The Woman's Bible* adapted the Revised Version in a translation by Julia Smith, a woman from Connecticut who had gained fame for refusing to pay property taxes because she was not permitted to vote.

Stanton witnessed much overt and covert opposition to feminism within the church hierarchy, as expressed by an all-male clergy. "All men pay more respect to the black coat than to any other," she wrote (quoted in Banner, 156). About male clerics, she noted, "Facts will show that no men, with few exceptions, behaved worse on our platform, and from no source did we have, and do we have today, such opposition as from them" (quoted in Banner, 157). While acknowledging Protestant flexibility, and even publicly thanking those ministers who invited her to speak from the pulpit on the issues of women's role in society, she spoke relentlessly against women's inequality as portrayed in the Bible.

Stanton believed that the real brunt of the opposition she faced came from those who could not reconcile her convictions about women's rights, which were self-justifying, with their own Christian beliefs and traditions. As she described it in 1880, "For twelve years in succession I have travelled from Maine to Texas trying by public lectures and private conversations to 'teach women to think.' But the chief obstacle in the way of success has everywhere been their false theology, their religious superstition. . . . Go into any little country town and the women's chief excitement is to be found in church fairs and church decorating" (quoted in Banner, 158).

Stanton's biographer, Lois Banner, observes: "By the 1890s she roughly outlined a feminist cosmology. In her view God was feminine as well as masculine, the apex of a system of male and female forces which permeated the universe and kept it in equilibrium. Among human beings, this system took the form of sexual attraction between men and women and provided that women were drawn to a patriarchal God and men to a maternal one" (159). Stanton posited that "The reason we have an exclusively male God is that our religion is . . . sustained mainly by women" (quoted in Banner, 159).

She did not accept the divinity of Christ, nor the virginity of his mother, "a slur on all natural motherhood." She regarded Christ as the "great leading Radical of his time." For her, the Old Testament was a patriarchal record, a history of "war, corruption, rapine, and lust" (quoted in Banner, 163); a reflection of masculinity at its worst. Meanwhile, an increasing number of women were now studying theology and asking to be ordained as ministers. Antoinette

Brown Blackwell, an old colleague of Stanton's, became the first ordained woman preacher.

Stanton became a mature thinker at the very time that the sons of the Enlightenment were also producing all-inclusive theories of historical and social development and utopianism, which, for the most part, pointed to the potentially infinite moral and intellectual progress of individual human beings and of the human race. In England, Herbert Spencer's work put evolution into social terms and, like Stanton, severely criticized traditional Christianity. Spencer's emphasis on the absolute rights of individuals and the consequent need for appropriate education, discipline, and self-control found some resonance in Stanton's evolving feminist philosophy of "self-sovereignty."

Bachofen's *Mother Right,* published in 1861, also helped to illuminate Stanton's understanding of social history. Bachofen theorized that there was a period in human history of undifferentiated sexual roles, then a period of matriarchy, followed by the stage of patriarchy in which the nineteenth-century was still embedded. Stanton suggested that women had been the first agriculturists because of their need for security and stability during pregnancy and nursing, and that it was women who gradually developed the kind of pre-dictable, peace-loving civilization wherein education, litera-ture, and the arts could flourish.

The patriarchal stage was a result of men having devel-oped superior weapons and a greater willingness to use force. When Stanton realized that there once had been a woman-centered civilization, she became fortified in her critique of the current patriarchal one, itself influenced by the story of Eve's mythic downfall (Banner, 86–87). She invoked often the concept of the *amphiarchate,* the anthropological term for an androgynous society in which social and professional roles are earned or granted entirely on the basis of ability, not sex. Because children would thus be raised with no hidden biases as to specific gender casting, all sex stereotyping would be eliminated and true democracy achieved.

In her later years, Stanton published essays and gave addresses on prison reform, labor strikes and unions, and the disparity between classes produced by increasing industrialization. In visiting utopian communities in England and the United States and in reading socialist writers, she was especially taken by the vision of the French thinker Auguste Comte, whose vision of a "religion of humanity" seemed to meld with her own mature sociopolitical thinking. As if to enact this vision, on several occasions during the 1860s, '70s and '90s, Stanton sought ways to create political coalitions among feminists, workers, and blacks. She challenged the National American Woman Suffrage Association to enrich its single goal of women's suffrage and to call for the reworking of the curriculum of schools to "inspire liberty and equality" in all relations in life, not just between men and women.

Stanton said that women are held in slavery by their constant fear of rape. "She recommended that every woman buy an immense Newfoundland dog for protection and carry a gun and learn to use it. Asked by dress reform groups once again to endorse the bloomer costume, she refused, replying that women, for safety, ought to adopt male attire and wear suits, coats, and trousers" (Banner, 107).

Elizabeth Cady Stanton was in the vanguard of those women who articulated the political and social implications of motherhood. "It is not in conventions . . . that our best work begins," she noted. "The radical reform must start in our homes, in our nurseries, in ourselves." She gave motherhood a special status, emphasizing its life-affirming, creative aspect. "As mothers of the race there is a spiritual insight, a divine creative power that belongs to women." Likewise, she observed that it was impossible "to work out any general reform in any department, until we can raise up a new race of women" (quoted in Banner, 75, 84).

Stanton affirmed publicly that she enjoyed the sexual relationship. Her position on birth control remained rather ambiguous. Some of her writings indicate that she might have been ignorant of the practical methods of birth control, others suggest that she was informed and approving but did not practice them herself. Elisabeth Griffith concludes that Stanton, the mother of seven children, did not practice birth control (65). Griffith calculates that during the seventeen-year span of Stanton's child-bearing years, she became pregnant each time Henry was at home for any length of time when she was not breast-feeding.

On the matter of abortion her position was clear. She castigated abortions as "disgusting and degrading crimes," (quoted in Griffith, 133) though she did not condemn women who had them performed. She believed most unwanted pregnancies were the results of men's oppressive sexual license, and counseled women to beware of ill-motivated seductions by men (Griffith, 133). She often spoke of the insidious fact that the frequency of intercourse had been always controlled by the husband. The wife should seize control of her own body, she suggested.

Stanton frequently asserted in her addresses that with dynamic education reform, including the institution of coeducation with a common curriculum for males and females, the class structure would even out and become more democratic. She was also emphatic about the need for what she called "moral education," which she thought more important than the teaching of practical skills.

On election day, November 2, 1880, when a wagon stopped outside her home in Tenafly, New Jersey, offering a ride to the polls for eligible male voters, Stanton called out that she was a tax-paying property owner and intended to vote herself. Both she and the visiting Susan B. Anthony went to the polls that day, where, Griffith says, "Stanton explained to the inspectors . . . she was three times the legal voting age, she had been a resident of Tenafly for twelve years, she had paid the real estate and poll taxes . . . she could read and write. . . . Unmoved by her litany, the men would not let her put her ballot in the box, so she hurled it at them. 'The whole town was agape with my act,' she bragged" (171).

Following her husband's death in January 1887, Stanton

traveled widely in Europe and across the United States visiting her children. In 1891 she moved for the last time back to New York City, where she lived with her son Robert, a lawyer, and her recently widowed daughter, Margaret Lawrence, a professor of physical education at Columbia Teachers College. Susan B. Anthony had wanted her friend to come live with her in Rochester.

Six thousand people celebrated Stanton's eightieth birthday at the Metropolitan Opera House in New York on November 12, 1895. Dressed in black silk and white lace, she sat in a red velvet chair awash with red roses, her name spelled out in a massive garland of carnations and chrysanthemums behind her on stage. She was almost unable to walk, given her obesity and the infirmity of her age, but she graciously received the acclaim of national and international women's groups. (Mormon women gave her an onyx and silver ballot box that could not be opened, amusing the honored guest.) Stanton hobbled to the podium with the help of two canes and one of her children at each arm, and to thunderous applause she said only, "I am well aware that all these public demonstrations are not so much tributes to me as an individual as to the great idea I represent — the enfranchisement of women" (quoted in Griffith, xiii).

Though she was of strong constitution, Stanton nevertheless had begun to falter physically in the 1890s. But she continued to read and to write, and toward the very end of her life she was preparing to put out an edition of her speeches. She died in October 1902, totally blind, in the apartment she shared with two of her children, having been fashionably dressed and her hair fixed by her daughters Margaret and Harriot. She stood at a table for several minutes with hands folded, then sat back down and lost consciousness forever.

The relationship of Elizabeth Cady Stanton and Susan B. Anthony survived the tumult of fifty years of intense reform politics, but some philosophical tensions lingered between them during the late 1880s and '90s. Anthony had not liked *The Woman's Bible*. And because of her single-issue focus, she had much more successfully retained the support of the more conservative elements in the women's suffrage movement, becoming president of the National American Woman Suffrage Association after Stanton's 1892 resignation. One of the two friends' final joint projects was to work to admit women to the all-male University of Rochester.

Referring to Lucy Stone, mainstay of the American Woman Suffrage Association, and her long-time friend Susan B. Anthony, Stanton observed, "Lucy and Susan alike see suffrage only. They do not see a woman's religious and social bondage, neither do the young women" (quoted in Banner, 154).

Consistently throughout the 1850s and 1860s, often almost alone, the team of Stanton and Anthony had fought for suffrage, divorce reform, and the rights of working women. As Stanton described their early partnership, "I forged the thunderbolts, and she fired them" (quoted in Banner, 59). Paradoxically, Anthony has become better known as the primary suffragist. In November 1977, a meeting convened in Houston to observe International Woman's Year opened with the arrival of a torch carried by women from Seneca Falls. Susan B. Anthony's grandniece was there on stage, and it seemed that the memory of Elizabeth Cady Stanton had been entirely lost. Likewise, in July 1923, the seventy-fifth anniversary of the Seneca Falls Convention, a program was planned in Seneca Falls to introduce an Equal Rights Amendment. The program made no mention of Elizabeth Cady Stanton. However, Stanton's daughter Harriot insisted on speaking about her mother. The ceremony culminated with a motorcade to Susan B. Anthony's memorial in Rochester, where a wreath was laid (Griffith, xv).

But clearly it had been Elizabeth Cady Stanton who set the courageous feminist agenda of the nineteenth century, wrote its documents, articulated its philosophy, and imparted the vision of the feminist movement as it lit the way to the passage of the vote-granting Nineteenth Amendment on August 26, 1920. According to Griffith, Stanton was the "most important foremother of the nineteenth century." She had "the intelligence, energy, vision, and courage to be a heroic character, and she was. She marshalled her superior qualities in a daily battle against entrenched institutions that denied women their social, economic, and legal independence. She was defeated again and again and again, but she continued the struggle with passionate impatience" (xix).

Stanton wrote that the ballot alone could not accomplish the liberation of women in the most fundamental sense, but only "a revolution in society, politics, and religion" (quoted in Banner, 88). Precisely as a feminine force for that kind of socially inclusive revolution, Stanton survives as a marker for my journey toward healing and self-realization.

CHAPTER FIVE

~~~~~~

Departure:
The Male Compass

The women's rights convention held in Akron, Ohio, in 1851 was particularly boisterous, punctuated frequently by the blustery speeches of incensed male ministers offended by the clamor for women's liberation. Sojourner Truth, a former slave and eloquent advocate for abolition and women's rights, rose in the midst of the melee and walked to the front of the room. In her resonant voice she said, "Well children, I think that twixt the niggers of the South and the women at the North, all talking about rights, the white men will be in a fix pretty soon" (quoted in Evans, 104).

I have found that once white males, politically and personally, grant the mythic importance of the lives of Elizabeth Cady Stanton and Frederick Douglass, they face the need to redefine themselves, all the way down to the solitary roots of their individual realities, just as Elizabeth Cady Stanton would have it. I know this from experience. We become responsible for our own destinies and find ourselves embarking on journeys to redefine our respective lives. In those journeys, we must be sure to map in particular the terrains of love, heroism, and our relationship to peoples of color.

In the late sixties and early seventies, when many women began to dress ceremonially without bras in a gesture of self-liberation, I found it rather puzzling that the erect nipples I could then discern through their skimpy T-shirts were titillating beyond belief. It was ironic that women who were adamantly opposed to being sexual targets — their sexual slavery symbolized by those lacy breast harnesses — had actually made themselves more alluring. I don't think that many women understood this at the time but, in any case, the suggestion of the nipple under any garment sent my imagination into overdrive.

During this same time period, I could neither accept nor surrender to the images of the Vietnam War as they played on television each night on national news. The good guy part of me, the product of the training provided by Roy Rogers and Wild Bill Hickok, wanted to help out, wanted the camaraderie implied by the military life. I had grown up with its legacy, acted it out in sports, and immersed myself in its tacit values for twenty years of my life.

This, I suppose, is one of the strands of the fabric of what it has meant for thousands of years to be a man in society. The physically stronger male sex, who could swing axes the hardest, hurl spears the farthest, and kill most swiftly, has always known how to affirm its supremacy by putting on war paint or a uniform and facing the dangers of the enemy. And certainly wars have served to protect home and hearth, on one side of the line or the other. Indeed, who is to say that war has not been always inevitable, necessary, and sometimes just? There is, of course, an industry of scholarship that combs history for incidents of subterfuge and arcane details that reduce war to personal jealousy and trivial misunderstandings. Nevertheless, war has been with us for ages, and the military has always been a major vehicle by which men have asserted their masculinity.

And for men to assert their masculinity has meant to act sexually. As I grew up, the wink from an uncle, the magazines of undressed females, the bragging rights earned by French kissing and other forms of conquest all contributed to a powerful mythology about the meaning of women. Girls and women became tantalizing creatures whose underwear was far more important than pages from the Bible, whose budding breasts contained volts of magic, and whose shy smiles were secret codes for potential sexual splendor.

The thought of women's pubic hair, or even underarm hair, the naked skin of their buttocks, what they might look like taking a bath, all seemed to coalesce into a too-dazzling dream that would surround me with longing almost every minute of every day. Women were to attract, to kiss, to get undressed, and to do one's horny will upon — this was the nature of girls and women. They were thrilling territory that it was my right to explore and conquer and into which I should, in the name of manhood, necessarily plunge my hungry flag.

I liked girls who were vulnerable, girls who liked me, girls I could manipulate and string along. I liked girls who needed me, because I didn't need them. I was not aware of any need that I might have to express love or respect to a girlfriend. I required that they like me first and that they permit me to act like a man and let me have my free will and my rooster rights to prance without needing anyone or anything — that I would admit to. I was quiet and attractive, and I held secrets that I was not even aware I contained. Women liked me. They liked strong men, and they took my silence as strength. This dynamic permitted them to be silly and giggly, and we guys liked that, we who could play basketball and football and be buddies without even needing each other.

Somehow boys learn to be quiet, at least quiet about their needs. It probably gets passed through the genes, this assignment to suffer quietly, to play while hurt, to brush off the pain and go forward in the hunt because your brothers in the hunt require it of you. And it is not a bad way of life. There is much bravery and drama in being this kind of a man.

The military is still ostensibly the male fortress for physical strength and the protection of women and children. Warfare has changed radically, enemies shift, and increasingly coalitions of educated men and women condemn war and violence, but violent threats to the state, real or imagined, still require the intervention of armies.

And whether one likes it or not, men still get hot for women. There is always that call of the sexual beast, the loon cry of longing for the sexual act, the nitty-gritty hands-on roll in the hay, when the fire crackles to a pitch that requires the application of the suck and kiss of waters down under and deep within.

On this level, one cannot get much closer to the hearth fire that burns perpetually in the marrow of the male than this deep-down pounding to be expressed naked with a woman. For the most part, feminist theory does not allow men to be turned on by the curve of a woman's body, by the subtle motion of a breast, or the way a woman with a coffee cup in her hand turns her head when she talks.

There is no word in the feminist dictionary for the deep dish signal of a woman's body as it is received in a man's heart, or wherever he receives it. And I realize that this is precisely the point. Where does a man receive and process a woman's sexual vibration? Certainly, if men receive it merely intellectually, male desire poses no real threat to womanhood, because it remains abstract. But if women are understood to be only sexual and woman's being is translated merely sexually into the googling wasteland of a man's cravings, women are degraded and justly infuriated. Then women become one-dimensional players whose faces, whose hair, whose shoes, and whose handbags all become merely sexual. This is what women are rightly frightened and angry about.

If men engage in sexual intercourse with women whom they regard only as objective, physical bodies, without the slightest love or respect, then intercourse is deemed rape, and rightly so. But feminists, trying to sustain a sense of their own sexual will and sexual dignity after thousands of years of subjugation, are not particularly interested in acknowledging or even exploring men's hot-blooded attraction to women.

My point here is to try to redeem — if contemporary men and women can accept that word — the raw, spontaneous, whitewater buzz that forever sends its vibration out toward women, especially as our sexual energies mingle with our intellectual and spiritual drives.

Like Robert Bly, I observe that men of the last twenty-five years have changed dramatically, perhaps for the better, becoming softer, gentler, more apt to be sensitive to the needs of child care, keener to enter into equal partnerships with women, more likely to trim the bravado they inherited culturally but no longer really own. I understand Bly to say that men are much nicer and further along on their journey to becoming equal and civil partners in the human enterprise, but that they are still missing something (Bly, 1–4).

It may be true that men of the last quarter-century have come to stifle and disavow the thrust of their animal sexuality, along with the horny will to know and love and create, deferring to the cumulative persuasion of women warriors. But it is neither honest nor courageous of men to acquiesce to feminist demands merely by capping the dizzying, multifaceted sexual impetus. More befitting of the search for masculine self-realization is for us to attempt to reclaim sexuality at its male sources, and then to think and work hard to find its proper direction.

Whatever the relative weight we choose to put on the sexual dimension alone — and it is certainly easy to grant it too much, given its pervasiveness in the popular culture — we must acknowledge that our sexual feelings provide a vitality that informs everything we do in the work of civilization, including making love. Without sexuality, we lack full mind, heart, and spirit. The expression of one's sexuality is, ultimately, a moral issue, but to disclaim one's sexuality out of some kind of fear or deference to feminism is to strangle a crucial impetus of self-realization.

As a young man, I thought about women all the time. I watched them, I imagined them naked, I listened for mysterious clues in everything they said. But to have a relationship with a woman that was a friendship was perhaps the most threatening thing I, or any man, might do. Sexuality in and of itself is nothing more than one of hundreds of boxes males can hide in, and I believed that if I were known to a woman on a daily, familiar basis, if I were to be open about my hesitancies, fears, and disappointments, I would feel less of a man. So I did my best to remain aloof from women, even from my wife. She, I know, saw this as peculiarly male behavior, a strange form of torture I was inflicting on her and on myself. I don't know how she tolerated my aloofness for as long as she did. But I think she understood that it was based on fear and that I should therefore be pitied more than anything.

My wife was right in understanding my behavior to be a form of fear. But I had no place to turn for its exorcism. I kept my emotional distance, and each of us suffered through as well as we could. I had always felt sexual desire as it reached out like a high-tension wire to random, walk-by women whom I possessed only in my imagination. To become actually intimate with a woman would be to risk being naked, revealed, a state that was apparently much easier for women to attain, especially with each other. The problem of reaching out in love, friendship, and relationship to women or men seemed to me to be an insoluble one. How could one offer the very substance of one's lifeblood, one's indivisible self-sufficiency, to others and not thereby be diminished? Through hard experience, I know the answer lies in the strengthening of men's feminine aspect.

A man's feminine side consists of the softer, subtler talents of relationship-building, of intuition, of nurturance, of the genuine ability to understand and communicate. For just as women have been undervalued in religion, social life, and under the law, so the feminine side of men likewise has been suppressed, kept under wraps, put down and out of sight. If men could break the mold of the solitary, reticent male, who depends on the female exclusively for emotional and sexual housework, and could develop their own feminine and relational reservoirs, we would have a more mature and harmonious society. At the very least, the intensity of the sexual union is deepened and diffused throughout the heart and mind when two human beings stand equally naked in relationship to each other.

Women, likewise, have a masculine aspect. The feminist movement has been an evolution toward women's acquiring the more overt, more masculine-associated, more abstract capacities for self-expression historically attributed to men. So while women have won the right to vote and have increasingly emerged as fully empowered political and professional players in modern society, it seems equally apt for men now to acknowledge their own feminine aspect and to develop, honor, and express it.

If I have grown in my ability to relax the sexual hypervigilance that for most of my life seemed necessary and inevitable, it has been with the recognition that the more subtle, more feminine aspects of the need for relationship and the ability to feel has to increase in its vigor and become co-equal, at least, with the pure, sometimes rapacious, sexual drive. For me, Elizabeth Cady Stanton is the embodiment of an eloquent and forceful feminine that clearly demonstrates its necessary and inevitable ascendancy. In this sense, she is a fulcrum by which men can learn to balance the masculine and feminine.

But another aspect of what modern males are missing, aside from self-confidence and pleasure in their capacity for relationship and feeling, is a quality that has almost always sustained them: the willingness and necessity to go to war. We are part warrior. But we are living in an age in which the act of war has become deeply and forever suspect. With nuclear arsenals overflowing, with technology transforming warfare by removing it to a level that depersonalizes killing, we either forge a new social contract that would forbid large-scale conflict forever, or face the real possibility of self-annihilation. The ceremony of war has begun to disintegrate. No longer can one nation fight discretely against another. With high-speed weapons that circle the globe, the entire planet would become a participant in any modern war, and every nation would lose.

Thus, men have to find other avenues for earning their manhood rights. Boys will still have to be initiated by some encounter with danger and the cultivation of courage, but the violence they do and the enemies they slay will have to be of an entirely different order. To begin with, the events of Seneca Falls would suggest that males will have to earn their manhood by initiation into a new world in which men and women are equal, in which men honor their feminine as well as their masculine and sexual aspects. In a sense, we have to return to a kind of hand-to-hand combat with ourselves and with all the men and women we love. Instead of clashing in the old warfare, males must raise their swords in the building of community, local and global, in which they themselves are not victors, but cooperative equals. Men's new battlefield is men themselves.

But even such would-be radical, individual transformation is not enough. The realignment of love and heroism must take place within a circle of individuals, within a context of community, next to peoples of color. And here I stand in fear and proceed in ignorance. The circle is broken.

When I was in VISTA briefly during the late sixties, I lived with a black family in rural Kentucky. Five of the children were living at home at the time, and several others had grown up and left. It was a small house with lots of fold-out beds and an outhouse about fifty feet from the kitchen door. I remember the father, a husky, tall man shouting orders from inside the outhouse to his sons working in the family's massive garden down below. The garden was the hub of the daily work of this subsistence-level family, and the mother had an extensive pantry that contained the vegetables they had grown and canned.

I remember eating dinner there one evening on a large picnic table covered with a paper tablecloth, with biscuits and beans spread out and a large dish of hot peppers set near the father's place. He would chomp on them periodically between his commands and pronouncements. This county was dry, and he was rumored to do a little bootlegging.

The mother of the family was a giant of generosity. She fed me, from what must have been a severely limited larder, wonderful homemade biscuits, black-eyed peas, rice, various bean dishes, and sausages. I have never eaten better or more plentifully. After dinner I would smoke Lucky Strikes out on the front porch, chatting occasionally with the man of the house, who once drove me around the countryside in his car to show me off, I think, to some of his white friends.

VISTA specialized in working with rural people, usually uneducated in a formal sense, to assist them in making use of government-funded services and to devise working groups and advisory councils to promote civil rights at the local, county level. I had no political savvy and no passion to help the family acquire a refrigerator or put a phone in. I was more interested in having sex, smoking cigarettes, drinking wine, and howling at the moon in a kind of coyote loneliness, all of which I had been doing plenty of at college. After a total of only about six weeks, I decided VISTA was not for me, and I left.

As I consider my life with this family, I know I glimpsed something terribly precious. I was witness to the lives of an ordinary family in rural Kentucky who were giants of the earth. The amount of work required to raise that number of children, work the garden, can food, and maintain the level of sanity and control which the family, especially the mother, demonstrated was truly inspiring, and I will never forget it.

I must point out that I had no real awareness at the time of what it meant that this was a black family and that I was white. At this stage of my social and emotional development, I was ignorant of the huge gap that existed between white and black cultures in this country, especially the profound extremes that existed in this rural Kentucky town. This kind of rose-colored, Disneyland view of reality, of which I was guilty, was common during the sixties, especially among college kids. In the minds of the sixties generation, especially among middle-class white kids who had been raised by Buffalo Bob and Zorro, racism would dissolve in the face of mere friendliness. Like them, I probably understood the concepts of racism and prejudice intellectually, but I had not come to understand fully their blood-stained economic, political, and social embeddedness.

In the early seventies, during one of my dropout times from college, I took up with a beautiful young woman, Anna, whom I would eventually marry. She was working in a bank in Rochester, New York, and we rented an apartment in a black neighborhood in Rochester, near Plymouth Avenue, on Troop Street. Our landlady was black, and with the exception of several hippies on the street, our neighbors were black. We encountered many black people as we shopped together or walked to and from events at the University of Rochester, across the Genesee River. One afternoon, we went to hear an elderly black bluesman, Sun House, play solo at the University. Some hours after the concert, and after it had become dark, Anna and I got into a spat. She decided to walk back to Troop Street, across the river, leaving me with the car. She huffed off into the night in the direction of our apartment, while I had to walk about a mile in the other direction to get the car.

As I drove home, I passed a soul food restaurant and noticed Sun House, who by now was feeling the effects of the liquor he had been sipping during most of the concert. He was staggering a bit, talking to the night-life crowd outside the restaurant. I stopped the little red Volkswagon I was driving, which belonged to Anna, rolled down the window, and shouted out an offer to drive him home.

He accepted and directed me down side streets until we arrived in front of his apartment. Then he reached into his pocket and pulled out a hefty wad of bills, obviously cash payment for his work that night, and offered to pay me. I said it wasn't necessary. He got out of the car with some difficulty, said thank you, and crossed the street.

Arriving home, I discovered that Anna had not yet returned, so I waited near the front porch. Perhaps a half-hour later, a long, low car, filled with black men, pulled up. As I watched, Anna emerged from the car. We went inside and continued our argument, but I still remember the unease I felt, which I did not mention to Anna, having seen her in this car filled with black men. I don't think I identified my feeling as a sexual thing, for I wasn't really sophisticated enough yet to put such matters into sexual or racial terms. It was just a generalized feeling of fear that Anna had been at the mercy of this group. They could have been a gang, for all I knew. They could also have been a group of neighbors returning from a local school meeting. But I felt an inexplicable fear and hatred of this car and its occupants. They were black, unknown, and, I guessed, probably did not conform to whatever conventions I had come to understand as the proper rules of life. Yet nothing unpleasant had happened during that car ride, and Anna had told me she was happy to have been offered it.

I did not know a single black person in my home town of Seneca Falls. At least one black family lived there as I grew up; their last name was Robinson. The son was three years ahead of me in school. I remember being aware of him, but I did not know him. During college, I didn't have a single black friend, not even a black acquaintance. With very few exceptions, I have observed black people pretty much from afar for most of my life.

When I was in graduate school at the University of Massachusetts, I met a young black man who was studying for his doctorate in English. He and I talked together about his difficulty in reading literature written predominantly, if not exclusively, by old white men. A talented writer, Steve's passionate pain was over his task of trying to grind out academic papers week after week on works written by people with whom he felt no cultural affinity.

In my Amherst living room, the feeling he expressed shimmered as if it were alive. His intensity and honesty, and his voice, which seemed to come from deep within, connected-him to me. But I saw him only on a few more occasions before I finished my program and my wife and I left town. At the time, I was too much an unconscious subscriber to the aloof school of manhood to even realize that here, sitting in my living room spilling his guts out, was a good man and a possible lifelong friend.

I have known few other black people during the last twenty years. One taught at a well-known boarding school in the Northeast, and identified himself as a Marxist. He continues to hone his craft as a writer, a gentle, smart young man desperately trying to nurture his own strong vision of economic justice in America, while maintaining the role of educator to privileged whites. He is kind and devoted, a person of tremendous integrity.

I know he felt a certain trepidation as a black man when he visited my family in western Massachusetts, sometimes arriving at night. One particular night, after we had moved from one house to another in a small rural town, he had difficulty finding our house. He told me later how scared he had been asking for directions. And he'd rehearsed all kinds of stories, excuses to offer, should he be stopped for driving around near midnight in that bucolic part of the world.

And then there is the black woman of about fifty whom I have known for some time. She is exuberant and direct, and she probably pitied me at the time of our first meeting, in Amherst in 1975, because I was still so naive, so completely isolated from the nitty-gritty of black-white relationships. On several occasions she, my wife, and I, along with other friends, have achieved an intimacy of understanding that for the hours we were together talking dissipated whatever racism may have lingered in our hearts.

I realized that the conventions that define the aesthetics of white faces are not the same for black faces. I began to realize how much racism depended on the definition of the "other" as ugly and inhuman. When I thought about it, I woke up to the fact that the great majority of advertising images are based on the white female face and that, of course, traditional movie stars inevitably reinforce the ideal of the human face as being white, often with blond hair and blue eyes, small noses, and even small teeth. Almost every magazine ad, every billboard, every television advertisement, except those for laxatives and air fresheners, were centered on the white face, often female, and the petite bodies attached to those faces.

I realized that a black person's face would never conform

to the standards of facial beauty as defined by white men and women and blatantly reinforced a million times a day in the media. So I began to think of white Americans' racism as a form of narcissism. As we white Americans came to love our own image as reflected in the golden pool of films and advertising, we were also losing our collective balance, losing any genuine relationship with peoples of diverse cultures and nationalities. Falling into the reflecting pond of narcissism, we were destroying ourselves.

During my graduate school days I read *The Autobiography of Malcolm X,* and *Native Son.* I began to understand racism in the gut, the terror and angst, the stunted lives it produces. Some of James Baldwin's writing in particular stunned me with its pained eloquence. I also began to understand that the experience of racism, in some paradoxical way, seemed to preserve and intensify in its victims the nuances and subtleties of being human. For when one's life is limited in some oppressive way by an outside agency, such as prison walls or the fact of prejudice, one's heart, if it is not destroyed, sometimes glows with a radiance that illuminates the intellectual and emotional presence of the human being. Baldwin, a targeted man in this sense, wrote with this power.

After I left graduate school and began working temporary jobs in small towns while trying to write and publish poetry and find a job teaching English, I felt the heartworm of racism. The older I became and the more clearly I was defined in the context of American society, the more difficulty I found in encountering black people with the same sense of open-hearted warmth as I would greet most white strangers whose path I might cross. I suppose that increasingly I began to walk like a white man, talk like a white man, and read and think like one.

As hard as I tried to apply my own understanding of the danger of narcissism as it laced white American society, I found myself succumbing from time to time to the opinion that black people lived on drug-infested, crime-riddled streets, scammed the welfare system, were unmotivated to work, and were dangerous.

Sometimes if I encountered a black person, or read about black people in the news, I would be aware of irrational, racist thoughts emerging from the front of my brain. Back in my more spiritual and sagacious brain, I would analyze this data, try to figure out the source of this racism, and attempt to annihilate it. This is something I continue to do. I still believe that racism has much to do with white Americans' singular narcissistic loyalty to their own mirrored artificial image. And in my spiritual brain, I still cling to the ideal that we are all human beings on this planet, marvelously diverse, and that we must overcome racism if we want to bring our society to full fruition.

While this ideal is immovable, set deep in my being like a bridge piling, I still feel some degree of culture shock when I see a black face. I still worry about the supposed sexual prowess of black men, even though I know it is a racist stereotype. I still spontaneously fear black neighborhoods as past the point of no return, with discourteous, unsupervised kids running the streets, and gang-infested schools. Most importantly, I feel uncomfortably vulnerable to black people. I feel like a hateful target of what I believe is their rage against white men in particular. I feel helplessly book smart, endowed with obscene amounts of leisure time, and shamefully immune from their suffering. And while I can intellectually understand how things got this way, I have very feeble tools with which to change the status quo. And there is the whisper in my breast that says let the black people save themselves — they don't want me or need me anyway.

The kind of flamboyant, ghetto lifestyle that some black people have grown up in, or have consciously chosen, makes me an outsider. The energetic music, the clothing, the air of bravado, the theatrical walk and hand gestures that have evolved among black brothers are fraternal codes used to create and maintain solidarity in the face of hated and dangerous white opposition. But they exclude me in a way that relegates me to the worst of that opposition. Sometimes when I pass a young, urban black man on a city street, the white-hot cool he projects simply wraps me in a contemptuous blanket. I understand this intellectually. As a representative of the white race, I deserve this contempt for being an ancestral participant in the institution of slavery and for being one of millions of whites who knows nothing about the hell of ghetto life, doesn't admit to being a racist, and does very little to work for a just society. All of this is probably written on my face, my clothes, the way I walk. I live trailing a giant shadow that is centuries long. I am not a recognizable change agent who speaks, writes, and acts for social justice.

Along with my feelings of fear and exclusion, I also experience a secret envy of blacks, even an inferiority. They appear bigger, stronger, more talented than I. Aside from the black poets, the artists, the architects, the doctors and lawyers who are merely competent at their respective trades, the black superstars of sports and entertainment seem bigger than life. They look beautiful. And they often speak out of an impressive depth of character that has been honed by adversity. Yet I sometimes feel inwardly uncomfortable when I fully acknowledge some of the remarkable black men and women of America.

But I happen to be a man from Seneca Falls. By exploring the house that Elizabeth Cady Stanton and Frederick Douglass put in order there in 1848, I hope to arrive at becoming a truly modern man, a person who is at least in a democratic relationship to women and blacks. A map of Seneca Falls would allow whites and African-Americans, men and women, to find their way back to the fires that combusted there more than one hundred years ago across racial, sexual, and social lines, and to be baptized into a society in which no race or sex dominates, but all exist in a circle around an American center.

CHAPTER SIX

Father Douglass

In the Wesleyan Chapel, at the corner of Fall and Mynderse streets, which was the site of the 1848 Seneca Falls Woman's Rights Convention, at least two important events happened: a woman publicly demanded the vote for the first time in American history, and a black man — legally free only since December 1846 — publicly supported her.

Of the approximately three hundred individual delegates to the convention, thirty-one were men, and of these men only Frederick Douglass spoke in favor of the specific resolution calling for the enfranchisement of women. Thus, on a holy spot in the sanctuary of a small church, traditions of centuries were quietly and miraculously killed. These two figures unmasked the hypocrisy of America's democratic rhetoric.

Frederick Douglass, a self-educated, relatively young man of thirty-two, was emerging as an important lecturer and writer in the abolitionist movement in the United States. His very presence at the Seneca Falls Convention represented the potential for the transformation of the men, women, and children deprived of freedom and education and degraded by the institution of slavery. Elizabeth Cady Stanton likewise embodied a promise of transformation: the potential emergence of half of the population of the United States as self-determining citizens. In tandem the two represented the liberation of all human beings from any shackles, any prejudices, and the promise of raising up a new civilization.

The Declaration of Sentiments penned by Elizabeth Cady

Stanton was read to the delegation and approved unanimously. Ten resolutions, including the demands for the right of women to personal and religious freedom, the right to testify in court, the right to own property and to claim their own wages, the right to education and equality in trades and professions, the right to equality in marriage, and the right to custody of their own children, were also approved without difficulty. The resolution demanding women's right to vote, however, met fierce resistance. Even Elizabeth Cady Stanton's own mentor, Lucretia Mott, had counseled beforehand, "This will make us ridiculous. We must go slowly" (quoted in Foner, *Frederick Douglass on Woman's Rights*, 13; henceforth referred to as *Rights*).

Stanton had consulted with Douglass before the resolution demanding women's suffrage was read, asking for his support. When the resolution seemed headed to defeat, Douglass's speech on its behalf riveted the audience and swung the vote. Years later, in a statement on the occasion of Douglass's death, Stanton said:

> He was the only man I ever saw who understood the degradation of the disenfranchisement of women. Through all the long years of our struggle he has been a familiar figure on our platform with always an inspiring word to say. In the very first convention, he helped me to carry the resolution I had penned demanding woman suffrage. Frederick Douglass is not dead. His grand character will long be an object lesson in our National history. His lofty sentiments of liberty, justice, and equality, echoed on every platform over our broad land, must influence and inspire many coming generations. (*Rights*, 41)

As editor of the antislavery publication the *North Star,* Douglass also ran a long editorial concerning the Seneca Falls Convention, on July 28, 1848. In part, it read:

> We are not insensible that the bare mention of this truly important subject in any other than terms of contemptuous ridicule and scornful disfavor, is likely to excite against us the fury of

bigotry and the folly of prejudice. A discussion of the rights of animals would be regarded with far more complacency by many of what are called the "wise" and the "good" of our land, than would a discussion of the rights of women. It is, in their estimation, to be guilty of evil thoughts, to think that woman is entitled to equal rights with man. Many who have at last made the discovery that the negroes have some rights as well as other members of the human family, have yet to be convinced that women are entitled to any. Eight years ago a number of persons of this description actually abandoned the anti-slavery cause, lest by giving their influence in that direction they might possibly be giving countenance to the dangerous heresy that woman, in respect to rights, stands on an equal footing with man. In the judgement of such persons the American slave system, with all its concomitant horrors, is less to be deplored than this "wicked" idea. It is perhaps needless to say, that we cherish little sympathy for such sentiments or respect for such prejudices. Standing as we do up on the watch-tower of human freedom, we cannot be deterred from an expression of our approbation of any movement, however humble, to improve and elevate the character of any members of the human family. . . . [W]e hold woman to be justly entitled to all we claim for man. We go farther, and express our conviction that all political rights which it is expedient for man to exercise, it is equally so for woman. All that distinguishes man as an intelligent and accountable being, is equally true of woman, and if that government only is just which governs by the free consent of the governed, there can be no reason in the world for denying to woman the exercise of the elective franchise, or a hand in making and administering the laws of the land. Our doctrine is that "right is of no sex." We therefore bid the women engaged in this movement our humble Godspeed. (*Rights,* 50–51)

While Douglass is far better known for his advocacy of the rights of black people, he worked at nearly the same spiritual frequency for women's rights. Indeed, the *North Star,* first published in December 1847, carried the slogan, "Right is of no sex."

Speaking before the International Council of Women in the 1890s, Douglass referred to his 1848 trip to Seneca Falls:

There are few facts in my humble history to which I look back with more satisfaction than to the fact, recorded in the history of the Woman Suffrage movement, that I was sufficiently enlightened at the early day, when only a few years from slavery, to support your resolution for woman's suffrage. I have done very little in this world in which to glory, except this one act — and I certainly glory in that. When I ran away from slavery, it was for myself; when I advocated emancipation, it was for my people; but when I stood up for the rights of woman, self was out of the question, and I found a little nobility in the act. (quoted in Foner, *Selections from the Writings of Frederick Douglass*, 23; henceforth referred to as *Writings*)

Two weeks after the convention, Douglass attended meetings in nearby Rochester to help ratify the program of the Seneca Falls Convention and spoke again in favor of the Declaration of Sentiments and its resolutions. There were few women's rights conventions during the next decade at which he was not present as an influential speaker. In one of his many statements extolling the civilizing effect women's participation would have in national and international affairs, he observed:

Nations have been and still are but armed camps, expending their wealth and strength and ingenuity in forging weapons of destruction against each other; and while it may not be contended that the introduction of the feminine element in government would entirely cure this tendency to exalt might over right, many reasons can be given to show that woman's influence would greatly tend to check and modify this barbarous and destructive tendency.

At any rate, seeing that the male governments of the world have failed, it can do no harm to try the experiment of a government by man and woman united. . . . I have never yet been able to find one consideration, one argument, or suggestion in favor of man's right to participate in civil government which did not equally apply to the right of woman. (*Writings*, 88–89)

During the frenetic period of debate leading up to the adoption, in 1869, of the Fifteenth Amendment to the Constitution, guaranteeing suffrage to black males, Douglass remained fiercely in support of women's enfranchisement as well, but thought it expedient not to tie black male suffrage to that of women at that time. On February 25, 1869, after receiving the necessary two-thirds vote in both houses of Congress, the Fifteenth Amendment was submitted to the state legislatures. Elizabeth Cady Stanton and Frederick Douglass exchanged strong words and were politically estranged during this national debate. Stanton and her colleagues withheld their support from the effort to pass the Fifteenth Amendment because it did not allow for the enfranchisement of women as well as black men.

Indeed, at the annual meeting of the Equal Rights Association in New York in May 1869, a majority of feminist delegates, including Stanton and Anthony, vociferously opposed the proposed amendment. In response, Douglass compared the cause of abolition to the cause of women's rights:

> When women, because they are women, are dragged from their houses and hung upon lamp-posts; when their children are torn from their arms, and their brains dashed upon the pavement; when they are objects of insult and outrage at every turn; when they are in danger of having their homes burnt down over their heads; when their children are not allowed to enter schools; then they will have an urgency to obtain the ballot equal to our own. (*Rights*, 33)

At the same time, Douglass fully affirmed his support of women's suffrage at this meeting, and expressed his regret that the Fifteenth Amendment would not grant it. In a resolution he introduced concerning the hope for the amendment's ratification, he asserted that it represented the "culmination of one-half of our demands" and asked the delegates to renew their "energy to secure the further amendment guaranteeing the same sacred rights without limitation to sex" (*Rights*, 34).

The Stanton-Douglass estrangement was not permanent. On the occasion of Stanton's seventieth birthday in 1885, Douglass wrote a note to *New Era,* a progressive magazine of the day:

> I make haste to ask an inch or two of your precious space, to join with her many friends in tendering sincere congratulations to Mrs. Elizabeth Cady Stanton on her 70th anniversary, and give her joy that she still lives, and that she is likely to tarry within the gates of life, long enough to see the fulfillment of her hopes and labors for the complete Emancipation and enfranchisement of woman. I am no stranger to the life and work of that excellent lady, and am proud to be one of the great cloud of witnesses who will on her 70th birthday, bear ample testimony to her high character as a woman, and to her immeasurable services to the cause of woman, as an advocate. Five and forty years ago in Boston, before the snows of time had settled upon the locks of either of us and before the cause of woman had taken its place among the reforms of the nineteenth century, Mrs. Stanton, then just returned from her wedding tour in Europe, sat by my side and taught me the new Gospel of woman's rights. I was then only a few years out [sic] Slavery, and I freshly remembered the lash and sting of bondage at the South, and the intense bitterness of the popular prejudice against color at the North, and was all the more ready to listen of such a beautiful teacher. Perhaps, no man is more a debtor to Mrs. Stanton for her noble work in the world, than myself. While she clothed woman in my mind with a dignity and grandeur which I had not before recognized, she gave me a higher conception of my own worth by disregarding popular prejudice and taking pains to impart to me the great truths with which her mind was illuminated. It is sometimes sad that women do not appreciate greatness in individuals of their own sex. I hope their utterances on the 70th anniversary of Elizabeth Cady Stanton will silence the slanders. Honor to whom honor. (*Rights,* 163)

Time and again, in his speaking and writing, Douglass grounded himself at the spiritual center of what human beings have valued since the Enlightenment as being just and noble with regard to human rights. In presenting his philosophy of relentless, moral fight, he took every opportunity to express the imperative need to think for oneself, forever advocating, as did Elizabeth Cady Stanton, that clear-headed and independent-minded men and women step forth from the mass of ordinary citizens and distinguish themselves with righteous action. For Douglass, to be a perpetual radical, or agitator, was the highest human role possible: one who thinks for oneself and goes beyond conventional lethargy to express righteously, morally, one's convictions.

Most males of the mid-1800s regarded women as domestic princesses who should leave brutalizing politics to men, who were considered better suited to such pursuits by virtue of their being naturally more mean-spirited and shrewd. Many of the same arguments used to uphold slavery were used to support male supremacy. Typifying contemporary male sentiment, the *New York Herald* asked, "How did women become subject to man, as she now is all over the world? By her nature, just as the negro is and always will be, to the end of time, inferior to the white race" (*Rights*, 12).

Men who supported women's rights were charged with being "Aunt Nancy Men" or "Hermaphrodites." This kind of opprobrium voiced by the ignorant seemed only to fuel Douglass's ardor. Referring to the badge of honor of being a "woman's rights man," he said:

> When the true history of the Anti-Slavery cause shall be written, women will occupy a large space in its pages; for the cause of the slave has been peculiarly woman's cause. Her heart and her conscience have supplied in large degree its motive and mainspring. Her skill, industry, patience, and perseverance have been wonderfully manifest in every trial hour. . . . Her deep moral convictions, and her tender human sensibilities, found convincing and persuasive expression by her pen and her voice. . . . Observing woman's agency, devotion, and efficiency in pleading the cause of the slave, gratitude for this high service early moved

me to give favorable attention to the subject of what is called "woman's rights" and caused me to be denominated a woman's-rights man. (*Writings*, 87)

Douglass often suggested that, in spite of heated opposition, by acting truthfully and righteously one earns a purified, transformed sense of self, a "pure flame of truth to burn up whatever hay, wood, and stubble it may find in its way. To be such a one is the deepest and sincerest wish of my heart" (*Writings*, 54).

The life and work of Frederick Douglass, like that of Elizabeth Cady Stanton, finally pivots on a principle of innermost revolution. If justice and equality and an end to prejudice are going to manifest, then things must change on both a political and a personal level. In an undated speech on women's suffrage, Douglass spoke of the revolution that would follow from granting full rights to women:

There is no question that if the demands of woman are complied with to the full extent to which she has been pleased to make them, we shall see a revolution, the most strange, radical and stupendous that the world has ever witnessed. It would equal and surpass that great struggle under Martin Luther for religious liberty.

At the beginning of this grand crusade, only a few women dared to stand forward and show their hand. It required a vast amount of conscience and surpassing courage to do so, but there were women equal to the occasion. . . . Against popular usage, against prejudice, against church, state, press, pulpit, platform, and the noisy tumult and abuse of the crowd, they rose in grandeur and glory alike the rainbow over the howling storm. (*Rights*, 134)

As noted earlier, Elizabeth Cady Stanton's influence was likened by one contemporary journalist to the blasting of guns and the thrusting of bayonets. Douglass noted:

Woman has already secured a vast vantage ground. Her voice and pen are both free. Archimedes only wanted a place for the fulcrum of his lever in order to move the world. Woman has found the place in her ability to speak, write, publish, organize and agitate. She has in this a weapon superior to swords, guns, or dynamite. No man even now, running for Congress or the presidency or any other office, wants to have the voice of the women against him. (*Rights,* 135)

A white woman and a black man became champions of two separate but deeply linked struggles that would revolutionize life in America. To the American white male, there could not be two more formidable, disconcerting foes. Elizabeth Cady Stanton embodies a revolution in his very house and Frederick Douglass a revolution in his public streets.

CHAPTER SEVEN

"Abolition Agitator and Ultraist":
The Moral Father of Democracy

Because abolition and women's rights posed such a powerful threat to entrenched male privilege, advocacy for them struck at the innermost nerve of the national psyche. Merely to espouse respect and admiration for reform in these two areas was dangerous enough, but to make active careers out of lobbying and agitating for them was heroic. Stanton and Douglass built their respective houses on volcanoes; the continuous and profound disapproval they attracted seemed to fuel them even more fiercely.

While Elizabeth Cady Stanton moved inward with time, toward the spiritual need to recognize and liberate the individual, Douglass moved outward toward the masses, lovingly and sternly chastising the American public at large. He was a perpetual reformer who lived, worked, and prayed in the house of political agitation:

> Let me give you a word of the philosophy of reforms. The whole history of the progress of human liberty shows that all concessions, yet made to her august claims, have been born of earnest struggle. The conflict has been exciting, agitating, all-absorbing, and for the time being putting all other tumults to silence. It must do this or it does nothing. If there is no struggle, there is no progress. Those who profess to favor freedom, and yet depreciate agitation, are men who want crops without plowing up the ground. They want rain without thunder and lightning. They want the ocean without the awful roar of its many waters. This struggle may be a moral one; or it may be a physical one; or it may be both moral and physical; but it must

be a struggle. Power concedes nothing without a demand.
It never did and it never will. . . . The limits of tyrants are
prescribed by the endurance of those whom they oppress.
(*Writings*, 61)

In addition to his commitment to social struggle, Douglass had a total spiritual devotion to realizing his own
potential. As a recently escaped slave living in New Bedford,
Massachusetts, he was unable to find work as a ship's
caulker, the work he had learned while in bondage in Maryland, because of resistance by white tradesmen. As a consequence, he worked as a general laborer, shoveling coal, dig-
ging cellars, loading and unloading vessels, and working the
bellows in a brass foundry. But: "Hard work, night and day,
over a furnace hot enough to keep metal running like water
was more favorable to action than thought, yet here I often
nailed a newspaper to the post near my bellows and read
while I was performing the up and down motion of the heavy
beam by which the bellows were inflated and discharged"
(*Writings*, 12, 13).

Frederick Douglass was born a slave in approximately
February 1817, in Talbot County, Eastern Shore, Maryland.
He never knew his white father, and he had been separated
from his mother who toiled in bondage about twelve miles
from where he lived as a young lad. He rarely saw her, but he
told the story of seeing her one night when she brought him a
gingercake, walking those twelve miles after her work on the
plantation had been done for the day. Douglass, seven at the
time, woke the next morning to discover that his mother had
left to hike back during the night. He did not remember ever
seeing her again.

Until he was about six, Douglass was raised by his grandmother; then he was taken to the residence of his master,
Captain Aaron Anthony, who managed the plantation of
Colonel Edward Lloyd (*Writings*, 9). Douglass remembered
being constantly hungry and cold, sometimes competing for
table scraps with dogs and cats.

At ten he was sent to live with Hugh Auld, a relative of Captain Anthony, where he worked for the next seven years as a house servant and as a caulker in Auld's shipyard. Auld's wife surreptitiously began to teach the young Douglass to read. When the master of the house discovered his wife's offense, he exclaimed in Douglass's presence that "learning would spoil any nigger." From that point on, Douglass understood the path to freedom. With money earned from shining shoes, he bought a school book called *Columbian Orator,* from which he garnered, in his words, "a bold and powerful denunciation of oppression and a most brilliant vindication of the rights of man" (*Writings,* 9–10).

In Auld's shipyard he continued to spin oakum, turn grindstones, and keep the fires under the pitch boilers. He practiced writing on the sides of ships, imitating letters and words he saw in his workplace.

Captain Anthony died when Douglass was sixteen, and the young slave became the permanent property of Thomas Auld, Hugh's brother. Concerned about a lack of malleability in his new slave's character, Thomas Auld turned him over to a professional "negro breaker," Edward Covey. From January to August 1834, Douglass was frequently overworked and whipped. After several heated encounters with Covey, a physical fight ensued, from which Douglass emerged the psychic, if not the physical, victor: "I was a changed being after that fight. I was nothing before, was a man now . . . with a renewed determination to be a free man. . . . I had reached the point at which I was not afraid to die. This spirit made me a freeman in fact, though I still remained a slave in form" (*Writings,* 10–11).

Douglass was soon transferred to a nearby plantation where he was better fed, and where he succeeded in teaching a secret Sunday school for the benefit of some of the slaves. After a failed attempt to escape, he was jailed briefly and then sent back to Baltimore, where he continued to work as a caulker in the shipyards.

In September 1838, when he was twenty-one, Douglass escaped, with the borrowed papers of a free black sailor in his pocket. He traveled by train from Baltimore to Philadelphia where, two weeks later, he was joined by Anna Murray, a free black woman he had met in Maryland, who came North specifically to marry him.

Douglass mailed the papers back to his accomplice, and he and his new wife settled in New Bedford, Massachusetts. Blacks could not attend the white churches of New Bedford unless they sat in separate pews with other blacks. So Douglass joined the black Zion Methodist Church, where he distinguished himself as a lay preacher.

He had been aware of the abolition movement since his enslavement in Maryland, and he now began to subscribe to its most prominent newspaper, the *Liberator,* edited by the tireless antislavery worker William Lloyd Garrison, and began to attend antislavery meetings in New Bedford, which were composed largely of black people. He met Garrison at an abolitionist rally there in 1841, and soon began to tour New England as an abolitionist orator, often working in tandem with Garrison himself and in association with other white antislavery advocates, such as Parker Pillsbury and S. S. Foster.

In one typical address on the abolitionist circuit, he recalled his days as a slave:

> In the deep, still darkness of midnight, I have been often aroused by the dead, heavy footsteps, and the piteous cries of the chained gangs that passed our door. The anguish of my boyish heart was intense; and I was often consoled, when speaking to my mistress in the morning, to hear her say that the custom was very wicked; that she hated to hear the rattle of the chains and the heartrending cries. I was glad to find one who sympathized with me in my horror.
>
> Fellow citizens, this murderous traffic is, today, in active operation in this boasted republic. In the solitude of my spirit I see clouds of dust raised on the highways of the South; I see the

bleeding footsteps; I hear the doleful wail of fettered humanity on the way to the slave-markets, where the victims are to be sold like horses, sheep, and swine, knocked off to the highest bidder. There I see the tenderest ties ruthlessly broken, to gratify the lust, caprice and rapacity of the buyers and sellers of men. My soul sickens at the sight. (*Writings*, 48)

His speaking territory broadened. In New Castle, Indiana, Douglass and his entourage were physically attacked. Beaten with a club and assaulted with racial epithets, Douglass almost lost his life.

For Douglass, slavery in the United States was

the granting of that power by which one man exercises and enforces a right of property in the body and soul of another. The condition of a slave is simply that of the brute beast. He is a piece of property — a marketable commodity, in the language of the law, to be bought and sold at will and caprice of the master . . . he is spoken of, thought of, and treated as property. . . . He is carefully deprived of everything that tends in the slightest degree to detract from his value as property. He is deprived of education. God has given him an intellect; the slaveholder declares it shall not be cultivated. If his moral perception leads him in a course contrary to his value as property, the slaveholder declares he shall not exercise it. The marriage institution cannot exist among slaves, and one-sixth of the population of democratic America is denied its privileges by the law of the land. What is to be thought of a nation boasting of its liberty, boasting of its humanity, boasting of its Christianity, boasting of its love of justice and purity, and yet having within its own borders three millions of persons denied by law the right of marriage? — what must be the condition of that people? (*Writings*, 45–46)

He diagnosed a moral sickness at the center of America.

The existence of slavery in this country brands your republicanism as a sham, your humanity as a base pretense, and your Christianity as a lie. It destroys your moral power abroad; it corrupts your politicians at home. It saps the foundation of religion; it makes your name a hissing and a bye-word to a mocking earth. It is the antagonistic force in your government, the only thing that seriously disturbs and endangers your Union. It fetters your progress; it is the enemy of improvement; the deadly foe of education; it fosters pride; it breeds insolence; it promotes vice; it shelters crime; it is a curse to the earth that supports it; and yet you cling to it as if it were the sheet anchor of all your hopes. Oh! be warned! be warned! a horrible reptile is coiled up in your nation's bosom; the venomous creature is nursing at the tender breast of your youthful republic; for the love of God, tear away, and fling from you the hideous monster, and let the weight of twenty millions crush and destroy it forever! (*Writings*, 52)

Douglass published his *Narrative of the Life of Frederick Douglass* in May 1845, with prefaces by Garrison and Wendell Phillips. And because the book named his former master, giving precise dates and places, Douglass became especially vulnerable to being arrested by bounty hunters and returned to Maryland. He therefore sailed to the British Isles where, for two years, he lectured on abolition and temperance in Ireland, Scotland, and England. While aboard ship Douglass was forced to sleep in steerage.

In responding to critics as a mature reformer, Douglass said:

You sneeringly call me an "abolition agitator and ultraist." Sir, I regard this as a compliment, though you intend it as a condemnation. My only fear is that I am unworthy of this epithet. To be an abolition agitator is simply to be one who dares think for himself, who goes beyond the mass of mankind in promoting the cause of righteousness, who honestly and earnestly speaks out his soul's conviction, regardless of the smiles and frowns of men. . . . To be such an one is the deepest and sincerest wish of my heart. It is part of my daily prayer to God, that he will raise up and send forth more to unmask a pro-slavery church, and to rebuke a man-stealing ministry — to rock the land with agitation, and give America no peace till she repent, and be thoroughly purged of this monstrous iniquity. While Heaven lends me health and strength, and intellectual ability, I shall devote myself to this agitation; and I believe that, by so acting, I shall secure the smiles of an approving God, and the grateful approbation of my down-trodden and long abused fellow-countrymen. With these on my side, of course, I ought not to be disturbed by your displeasure; nor am I disturbed. (*Writings*, 54–55)

Douglass returned from his overseas trip an international figure, and with money raised by British friends, purchased his freedom for $750 in December 1846. He founded the *North Star,* dedicated to the abolition of slavery, in Rochester, in December 1847, and it became the premiere antislavery publication, changing its name several times and remaining in circulation for sixteen years, the longest of any such journal. (Elizabeth Cady Stanton's cousin Gerrit Smith, an active abolitionist and reformer, helped Douglass financially in launching it.) During his career Douglass acted as a "conductor" and "station master" in the Underground Railroad in Rochester and frequently used his payments as a lecturer to help fugitive slaves.

Douglass broke with William Lloyd Garrison over the issue of the political strategy for abolition. Garrison wanted the Northern states to secede from the Union, asserting that the Constitution was inherently and irrevocably a proslavery document. This strategy, known as "moral suasion," was an appeal to the nation's sense of values and good judgement. Garrison disdained the use of the ballot and wanted the Northern states to establish their own separate charter, expressly annulling forever the institution of slavery. Douglass recognized that the Constitution did not advocate the practice of slavery and dedicated himself to harnessing its power to bind all of the states into a union that did not permit that institution anywhere within its borders.

Grounded in the moral strategy of the antislavery movement, he became politically active in the campaigns of the

Liberty Party, was appointed to their national committee in 1851, and remained allied to the Radical Abolitionists for the rest of his life (*Writings*, 28). In 1847, Douglass met John Brown, the abolitionist and eventual leader of the raid on Harper's Ferry, Virginia. Although he found Brown's arguments for the use of force to free the slaves compelling, the majority of Douglass's comments at this time were for peaceful political means.

In 1858, John Brown revealed to Douglass his plans for attacking the arsenal at Harper's Ferry. Douglass opposed the action (*Writings*, 29), but when Brown's attack, on October 16, 1859, failed, there was enough circumstantial evidence to implicate Douglass in the knowledge of the insurrection. Almost immediately he fled to the British Isles, and returned about six months later, when the consternation over Brown's armed siege had subsided.

During the Civil War, Douglass was a tireless advocate of recruiting black soldiers to fight for the cause of the North, and he directly assisted in the enrollment of the famed 54th and 55th Black Regiments from Massachusetts. His own sons, Charles and Lewis, were among the first blacks to join the Union Army. Rallying blacks to enlist, he said:

> The opportunity is given us to be men. With one courageous resolution we may blot out the hand-writing of ages against us. Once let the black man get upon his person the brass letters U.S.; let him get an eagle on his button, and a musket on his shoulder, and bullets in his pocket, and there is no power on earth or under the earth which can deny that he has earned the right of citizenship in the United States. I say again, this is our chance, and woe betide us if we fail to embrace it. (*Writings,* 72)

After the defeat of the Confederate States, during Reconstruction, Douglass became deeply involved in the work of reshaping the governments of the South to accommodate the freed slaves. Following Lincoln's assassination, former slaveowners began to regain control of the state legislatures and to reenslave blacks by restricting their civil rights. The freed slaves were landless and were not permitted to vote. Granted land after the war under Lincoln's administration, they were then stripped of it by order of President Johnson (*Writings,* 39). And so began Douglass's campaign to enfranchise black men, culminating in the Fifteenth Amendment, adopted by Congress in 1869.

> I expect to see the colored people of this country enjoying the same freedom, voting at the same ballot box, using the same cartridge-box, going to the same schools, attending the same churches, traveling in the same street cars, in the same railroad cars, on the same steamboats, proud of the same country, fighting the same foe, and enjoying the same peace and all its advantages. (*Writings,* 44)

Douglass campaigned for Gerrit Smith in his bids for the presidency, and was himself the vice presidential candidate on the Equal Rights ticket with Victoria Woodhull in 1872. In addition to his continuing work as writer and lecturer, Douglass went on to become president of the Colored National Labor Union, recorder of deeds in Washington, chargé to Santo Domingo, and minister resident and consul general to Haiti.

He died on February 20, 1895, just hours after attending a meeting of the National Council of Women, which Elizabeth Cady Stanton had helped found, in Washington, D. C. The *Rochester Democrat and Chronicle* of June 28, 1879, already had described him as "among the greatest men, not only of this city, but of the nation as well — great in gifts, greater in utilizing them, great in his inspiration, greater in his efforts for humanity, great in the persuasion of his speech, greater in the purpose that informed it" (*Writings,* 7).

How did America ever justify slavery and its terrible legacy? It was the black skin of Africans that originally shocked the English in their first contacts with the "dark continent" beginning in the 1500s. The color symbolism of black and white, as it suffused the art, literature, and religion of the

English, predisposed them to see the black faces of West Africans as embodiments of evil and sin.

According to the African-American scholar Richard Thomas, white and black connoted, respectively,

> purity and filthiness, virginity and sin, virtue and baseness, beauty and ugliness, beneficence and evil, god and the devil. Whiteness, moreover, carried a special significance for Elizabethan Englishmen: it was, particularly when complemented by red, the color of perfect human beauty, especially female beauty. This ideal was already centuries old in Elizabeth's time, and their fair Queen was its very embodiment: her cheeks were "roses in a bed of lilies." If one had to be lily-white with red cheeks to be beautiful, certainly then, the West Africans were nowhere on the English scale of beauty. (14, 15)

Thomas quotes Winthrop D. Jordan: "By contrast, the Negro was ugly, by reason of his color and also his 'horrid Curles' and 'disfigured lips and nose'" (15). Thomas goes on to say that by the time the slave trade had gained momentum in the 1600s, a growing racist ideology was also being imported to the New World along with hapless, chained, black human beings.

> The American Revolutionary War and the post-war period presented some problems of how the new nation would resolve the fundamental moral and political contradiction of holding slaves while preaching and fighting for freedom. As it would also successfully do in future situations, America fashioned a special brand of political and moral compromise that helped it to rationalize both the conquest of the native peoples as well as the enslavement of blacks. . . . Gradually an ideology emerged in America and Britain which explained that white racial dominance was a blessing. (17)

Among the forces in America that blessed the movement toward the dehumanization of black people was the enormous influence of Thomas Jefferson on the subject of race relations: "I advance it . . . as a suspicion only, that the blacks, whether originally a distinct race, or made distinct by time and circumstances, are inferior to the whites in the endowment both of body and mind" (quoted in Thomas, 19).

Many of the new nation's founding fathers were slaveholders, including George Washington. It is said that Jefferson's earliest memory is that of being carried about on a pillow by a black servant. Even his wooden coffin was built by a slave carpenter. And as Thomas notes, because Jefferson, whom he calls the first among America's ideological racists, was so beloved, so eloquent and so influential in his work to define the nature of a free society, his remarks about the inferiority of black Africans are etched deep in the American soul.

Jefferson feared black uprisings and exaggerated black sexuality. He feared that the arrogant and cruel example of slave masters would harden the hearts of young white boys, and he decried the loss of the sanctity of labor on the part of the white population. All these complaints regretted the negative effects of slavery on whites, not the horrible consequences for blacks themselves. Jefferson clearly pronounced blacks separate and unequal:

> It will probably be asked, why not retain and incorporate the blacks into the State? Deep-rooted prejudices entertained by the whites; ten thousand recollections, by the blacks, of the injuries they have sustained; new provocations; the real distinctions which nature has made; and many other circumstances, will divide us into parties, and produce convulsions, which will probably never end except in the extermination of the one or the other race. To these objections, which are political, may be added others, which are physical and moral. The first difference which strikes us is that of color. Is this difference of no importance? Is it not the foundation of greater or lesser share of beauty in the two races? (quoted in Thomas, 22)

Most other early American visionaries could not envision a nationhood of black, red, and white either.

Only the Quakers came close to this vision of a racially unified America. Jefferson and the majority of white Americans could only see the forceful expansion of white civilization over the land and bodies of red peoples with black people tucked away from sight or better yet, emancipated from slavery and shipped away to their African or Haitian homelands. (Thomas, 29)

Because there can never be a valid rationale for the enforced degradation of an entire people, those who acquiesced, either directly or indirectly, suffered a kind of disease of the spirit. Thomas says, "By its refusal to use moral forces to combat racial oppression against Indians and blacks, the white American Christian community lost its soul" (59).

Not surprisingly, therefore, the liberation of white males is contained in the problem of racism. Our true organization as human beings with fully liberated hearts and minds can not be entirely realized apart from the diverse community that America represents. And if I could choose the one black teacher who might bring me across that threshold from racial suspicion to an embrace of a truly diverse American community, it would have to be Frederick Douglass.

The modern poet Robert Hayden saw Douglass as a progenitor of a racially unified society.

FREDERICK DOUGLASS

When it is finally ours, this freedom, this liberty, this beautiful
and terrible thing, needful to man as air,
usable as earth; when it belongs at last to all,
when it is truly instinct, brain matter, diastole, systole,
reflex action; when it is finally won; when it is more
than the gaudy mumbo jumbo of politicians:
this man, this Douglass, this former slave, this Negro
beaten to his knees, exiled, visioning a world
where none is lonely, none hunted, alien,
this man, superb in love and logic, this man
shall be remembered. Oh, not with statues' rhetoric,

not with legends and poems and wreaths of bronze alone,
but with the lives grown out of his life, the lives
fleshing his dream of the beautiful, needful thing.

(*Collected Poems*)

It is against the issues of the black presence in America
and the abolition of slavery and the emancipation of women
that Frederick Douglass becomes a brilliant knife, cutting at
as if to heal the American soul. We do not find Seneca Falls,
nor do we find America itself, if we do not find him.

CHAPTER EIGHT

Shadows Across the Land

The insights of Carl Jung help us understand how racial and sexual prejudices evolve. Those human qualities which we, for one reason or another, find distasteful or sinful, Jung says, we assign to the shadow regions of our psyches, into the bag of our deep-down unconscious. This eviction of difficult elements of experience into rooms down below serves the conscious mind by making it appear to be, at least partially, in control.

The conscious mind can embody with relative ease a rational, linear agenda. Rational causes and effects, priorities, choices based on numbers and facts, all fall within the purview of the conscious, waking mind. Indeed, it is no accident that these areas are all pretty much the stuff of our modern technological society. The waking mind, its rational codes of control and behavior, its meshing with the details and schedules of life, operates much more successfully and efficiently if it is not hampered by the nagging, unpredictable, and sometimes irrational feelings that lurk beneath the neat corners and right angles of consciousness. Whatever resides within our unconscious somehow floats in darkness like an underground river.

Severe racial prejudice always flourishes in an artificially ordered and rigidly righteous neighborhood that the generic white man has claimed as his exclusive, well-swept country club of the mind. In America a narrow code of religiosity helped rationalize the institution of slavery and bless it with holy water. As long as black people are enslaved, or at least ghettoized and kept under the lock and key of racial prejudice, the mind of the dominant culture can move forward seemingly unaware. Likewise, questions of male and female sexuality, birth control, and frequency of sexual intercourse have for most of the last three hundred years been swept under the rug of America's waking religious and conscious life. Especially with regard to sexuality, the white society of America evolves from a rather strict code of moral behavior as carried by early Protestantism, hypocritical as it might have been.

Fully realized, joyous sexual energy and curiosity have nowhere to go for their full manifestation under these circumstances, and get put behind the psychic bars of our shadow places, especially next to black men. And because most white Americans (and this is conjecture) have not discovered ways of successfully integrating their sexual aspect with their waking lives, we begin to project our own illicit, unbaptized, sexual desires and insecurities — those that fall outside the carefully circumscribed regions of church-based values and the strict authority of the Ten Commandments — onto the backs of the black race, which we then render as despised and illegitimate.

Just as black people were forced during slavery to carry bags of cotton and haul barges and bricks and lumber, so they are made today to carry the unfulfilled sexual desires of white people who have not figured out how to become sexually integrated themselves. Even responsibility for the human capacity for violence, the lack of faithfulness to the family, and drunkenness and vice of all kinds is seemingly exiled from white consciousness and buried in the shadow. The dumping station of the ghetto is an American way of handling these unacknowledged aspects of ourselves, just as we send our toxic waste willy nilly to landfills in the backyards of strangers.

Now it is also true in literal fact that ghettos and inner cities are gardens of violence, of broken families, of neglected children learning the drug trade. And it is frequently true on a practical, experiential level that human beings of any color or ethnicity must be cautious in passing through certain black neighborhoods for fear that they might be robbed, beaten, or humiliated by wanton black marauders. The evidence is that violence, drug trafficking, and promiscuous sex do compose the daily agenda of the streets of inner cities.

And perhaps it cannot be otherwise at the present time. Nearly three hundred years of slavery, a decided lack of education, housing and job discrimination, the denial of civil rights, and a persistent, deadly racism have all worked their twisted will on the characters and destinies of black people in this country. The Constitution that failed to recognize slaves as citizens, the corruption of the Reconstruction period after the Civil War, the generations of quiet acquiescence of many of the nation's churches — all conspired to keep blacks in the shadow of the white race and in an unconscious codependence with them. And there millions of black people have remained, largely suffering, struggling, trying to find themselves, and, often at immense psychic costs, excelling in the narrowly limited fields grudgingly allowed them.

For the time being, on a societal level the conscious and the unconscious minds seem split almost irreparably over race relations. Most white people in America are cut off from any genuine dialogue with black people. As long as we live this way, nothing can happen in terms of our dynamic growth and fulfillment, either in the individual human psyche or on the level of politics. As long as whites and blacks, out of fear and unfamiliarity, choose to put up walls, as long as we live apart from communication with the energizing life of our shadows, we are condemned to stay fragmented and isolated. In separating ourselves from one another, we, both black and white, become like a mass of puzzle pieces doomed never to find each other, never to be made whole. As American society is presently constituted, we are primarily separate, and for one reason or another we keep missing each other.

Cornel West, professor of Afro-American Studies and the Philosophy of Religion at Harvard University, reflects on the question of leadership and how it might succeed in managing "black rage" in America while bringing this country to its democratic promise. He uses a jazz metaphor to express a dynamic vision of unity among diverse individuals.

> To be a jazz freedom fighter is to attempt to galvanize and ener-
> gize world-weary people into forms of organization with
> accountable leadership that promote critical exchange and
> broad reflection. The interplay of individuality and unity is
> not one of conformity and unanimity imposed from above
> but rather of conflict among diverse groupings that reach
> a dynamic consensus subject to questioning and criticism. As
> with a soloist in a jazz quartet, quintet or band, individuality is
> promoted in order to sustain and increase the creative tension
> with the group — a tension that yields higher levels of perfor-
> mance to achieve the aim of the collective project. This kind of
> critical and democratic sensibility flies in the face of any polic-
> ing of borders and boundaries of "blackness," "maleness,"
> femaleness," or "whiteness." Black people's rage ought to tar-
> get white supremacy, but also ought to realize that blackness
> per se can encompass feminists like Frederick Douglass or
> W.E.B. Du Bois. (105)

I am willing to approach the question of racism in American society, but I can do so only if I proceed in a way that
makes me feel relatively safe, under the auspices of a leader
whom I respect, if not love, and only in such a way that
ensures that I gain something either in terms of heightened
powers and prerogatives or some kind of palpable wisdom.
Racial unity is the only honorable dream available to us as
we think about the white and black elements of this nation,
both of which have been on this continent for about equal
amounts of time. When any of us, whether black or white,
talk about the merits of equal justice and equal opportunity,
we are really talking about a truly multiracial society, about
interracial marriage, about genuinely integrated schools and
neighborhoods, about multiethnic clubs and school boards,
about the browning of America.

Frederick Douglass, recently escaped from slavery, tacked

up a newspaper on the beams to read and further educate himself while working the furnace bellows with his hands. In the heat and sweat produced by foundry fires that transformed metal into liquid, he transformed himself into an agent of radical reform and into a true American advocate of justice and equality for all. It is my supposition that almost any white American who comes near to the heat and fire of Douglass's own radical soul-foundry of social change will also be duly heated and transformed.

As one of the most brilliant and courageous people of his century, Douglass also personifies the generalized black man in the unconscious shadow of the American psyche. In Jungian terms, he is the tall black figure who represents that which has been unfairly relegated to the shadowy places of the white man's unconscious, but in his case miraculously made articulate, powerful, and whole. He steps forth as a flesh and blood reminder, as a black man, of all that we have forgotten, decided to ignore, or are too afraid to admit about prejudice, racism, and the politics of race. And if we are not careful, we will imprison him in the shadow of history, where we glimpse him only from time to time, usually only during Black History Month.

In the same way, Elizabeth Cady Stanton, garbed in one of her favorite black silk dresses, represents another universal shadow figure for white and black men both: their feminine side. Likewise, given the extent that men feared women and found security and satisfaction in relegating them to second-class existence without civil or social standing, it took the towering figure of Elizabeth Cady Stanton to step out of the shadow of American life, out of both our individual psyches and the collective unconscious of American society itself, to call the question of sexual equality.

When shadow figures are as emphatic, consistent, and clear in their demands, as fair and humane as were Frederick Douglass and Elizabeth Cady Stanton, as capable of wit and good humor, as exemplary, what choice do we have but to immerse ourselves in the challenges they offer?

Douglass emerges even today intact from the rubble of ruined black lives, having survived the awful precincts to which America has relegated African-Americans. He emerges whole, righteous, eloquent, inspiring, a veritable hero for all to see. If we somehow deny the brilliant force of his example, we men cripple ourselves. We remain bifurcated in terms of our own personal unity of character, of our conscious and unconscious selves, and within society in its disparate black and white elements.

Douglass's heroism, his singular drive to speak out and write about the injustice of slavery and racism, equals or surpasses the force and beauty of anything envisioned or accomplished by the democratic will of Thomas Jefferson or Benjamin Franklin. And it is on the unlikely stage of Seneca Falls that the two shadow figures of Douglass and Stanton stood still in the flesh and changed America psychically if not historically at the moment of the First Woman's Rights Convention. Dynamic equality between men and women and between whites and blacks, and the dream of the self-determination and self-actualization of every human being intellectually, politically, and spiritually, were here inaugurated for all the world to see. We may not have literally heard Douglass support Stanton on Thursday, July 20, 1848, as she presented her bid for women's right to vote, or in his countless other briefs for the equality of blacks and women, but I believe all of us hear the reverberations of his words as they continue to disturb us.

CHAPTER NINE

Morality, Maps, and the Modern Hero

Our age is remarkable in its globe-shrinking, world-fragmenting forces, in its changing allegiances, in its suffering, in its technology, in the conflict between its races and religions, between male and female. We really do not know what values to nurture, what individual men and women to call heroes, what saving philosophy to invoke. Joseph Campbell, scholar of myths and heroism, speaks of the need for a societal map for our time.[1]

> Nor can the great world religions, as at present understood, meet the requirement. For they have become associated with the causes of the factions, as instruments of propaganda and self-congratulation. . . . Such a monkey-holiness is not what the functioning world requires; rather, a transmutation of the whole social order is necessary, so that through every detail and act of secular life the vitalizing image of the universal god-man who is actually immanent and effective in all of us may be somehow made known to consciousness. (389)

There is an observable dual process going on in our yet-to-become global community, destructive and creative, putting together and tearing apart. Any would-be hero would have to understand and master the dynamics at the deepest levels before inviting followers to safety and freedom. And

[1] Much of what Campbell says is cast in terms of masculine pronouns, as if to imply that the God-force can only be understood in terms of males. For our purposes here, of course, women are regarded as full candidates for heroism, and the Campbell quotations are used in a universal, male/female sense.

without heroes and torchbearers, we men and women and boys and girls are caught in a social, political, and spiritual riptide in which it is nearly impossible to keep a sense of sanity and balance. Ironically, as the world grows smaller and exposes us even more intimately to each other through technology, we somehow feel more and more invaded, more swept off our feet, increasingly disoriented and vulnerable. Without the old stone walls that separated right from wrong, the prejudices we inherited from our parents, and most of the natural boundaries that once defined our personal world, many of us are lost, without center or purpose.

Campbell observes that in the past, either the earth or the skies were the frontiers to which heroic men and women brought light, but that now we human beings ourselves, our hearts, minds, and spirits, are the field in need of the most passionate pioneering work. "The hero-deed to be wrought is not today what it was in the century of Galileo. Where then there was darkness, now there is light; but also, where light was, there now is darkness. The modern hero-deed must be that of questing to bring to light again the lost Atlantis of the co-ordinated soul" (388).

And he warns that "the problem is nothing if not that of rendering the modern world spiritually significant — or rather . . . nothing if not that of making it possible for men and women to come to full human maturity through the conditions of contemporary life" (389).

If Campbell is correct, we have to comprehend the present, dual destructive/creative process as happening individually, within our own breasts. And the imminent, revitalizing "hero-deed" for the spiritual healing of this civilization is the reclamation of the recharged and reoriented souls of individual men and women. For Campbell, the acquisition of an individual, "co-ordinated soul" is reflected and mapped by the development of the hero as portrayed in myths and tales. The cyclical event of the appearance, or process, of the heroic is at once simple and complex, fabulous and practical.

In Campbell's terms, not only are individual men and

women capable of managing the drama of the personal quest for heroic wholeness, but the stage of the modern world is actually set for the appearance of a greater spiritual hero or heroes, who will somehow illuminate and reorient the human soul itself as the highest and most necessary deed of our era. It is not heroic science or outward exploration that is required of Western civilization at this time in history, but the very rediscovery of what it means to be a human being and to have a soul. And time is running out.

> The modern hero, the modern individual who dares to heed the call and seek the mansion of that presence with whom it is our whole destiny to be atoned, cannot, indeed must not, wait for his community to cast off its slough of pride, fear, rationalized avarice, and sanctified misunderstanding. "Live," Nietzsche says, "as though the day were here." It is not society that is to guide and save the creative hero, but precisely the reverse. And so every one of us shares the supreme ordeal — carries the cross of the redeemer — not in the bright moments of his tribe's great victories, but in the silences of his personal despair. (390–391)

Campbell's map of the heroic journey is a familiarly human one.

> The hero . . . is the man or woman who has been able to battle past his personal and local historical limitations to the generally valid, normally human forms. Such a one's visions, ideas, and inspirations come pristine from the primary springs of human life and thought. Hence they are eloquent, not of the present, disintegrating society and psyche, but of the unquenched source through which society is reborn. The hero has died as a modern man; but as eternal man — perfected, unspecific, universal man — he has been reborn. His second solemn task and deed therefore . . . is to return then to us, transfigured, and teach the lesson he has learned of life renewed. (19–20)

Elizabeth Cady Stanton and Frederick Douglass fulfill Campbell's definition of world-changing heroism, and in their cooperative work in Seneca Falls, they show us the path of the "co-ordinated soul." In Stanton's work to empower and transform the individual woman, she guarantees the transformation of men, as well. And Douglass, in his moral warriorship, provides an axis of personal transformation that includes the multicultural community, local, national, and global. On another level, these two people embody fierce, indelible models of realized manhood and womanhood. By their inspiring examples, we ordinary wayfarers can bolster what has grown weak, tired, and lost in ourselves.

 ˙ In the partnership of Stanton and Douglass in Seneca Falls, the mythic, modern dilemma of masculinity and femininity, creation and destruction, fragmentation and healing is vivid. They presided over the simultaneous killing of the old order and the creation of a new era, a vision of a true, multicultural community, in which men and women are equally empowered, self-governing, and so unlikely themselves to oppress. In this way, they are powerful embodiments of Campbell's mission "of making it possible for men and women to come to full human maturity through the conditions of contemporary life."

CHAPTER TEN

Killing Deeds That Heal:
The Heroism of Elizabeth Cady Stanton and Frederick Douglass in the Sacred City

The heroic journey is expressed in three distinct phases: departure or separation from known relationships and accepted tradition; arrival at or initiation into the knowledge of some sought-after vision; and return home to the society that would reject but desperately needs what the hero has risked his or her life to achieve.

Elizabeth Cady Stanton's departure had its preparations in her wedding trip to London for the World Anti-Slavery Convention where she would be radicalized under the tutelage of Lucretia Mott. But it was her extended leave-taking from cultured Boston and her difficult sojourn in backwoods Seneca Falls that completed her separation from the American society in which male dominance and white supremacy held sway. The further demands she experienced there of caring for her children, and the crushing weight of women's second-class citizenship hit her hard, nearly breaking her robust spirit. In the mythology of the hero's development, often under such duress, under conditions of great struggle and loneliness, the eternal vision breaks through. In Seneca Falls, Elizabeth Cady Stanton arrived at that breakthrough and was initiated into a larger moral framework of personal power and the feminist vision of independent thinking and equality for women.

The classic hero follows such departure and arrival with a return. Stanton's return took the form of her relentless, feminist organizing, done in the face of constant rejection by a hostile and at best ambivalent American citizenry, beginning with the Woman's Rights Convention, and continuing for the rest of her life as a courageous speaker and writer. She returned with all her might to the work of opposing oppressive laws and social conventions and of educating the nation. She received other radical men and women at her home on Washington Street, traveled, wrote and lectured, and expressed, by her own example, within the confines of this unlikely place, the vision of a whole new way for men and women to be human. Following her dramatic stay in the straits of Seneca Falls, Stanton began to live and work as strategist and philosopher for wider audiences, nationally and internationally. The son of Horace Greeley, who met Stanton when she visited a cooperative community in Colorado, remarked, "She seemed to live in several centuries at once" (Banner, 89).

Certainly her life was not a fable. It did not contain "fabulous forces" or "supernatural wonder" in a fairy-tale sense. But in the face of iron resistance from the press, the general public, and the more conservative elements of the women's movement itself, she was able to summon almost supernatural strength, as though she was the designee of some mystical force. Freeing herself from the tentacles of current social customs and traditions, she acted out the way of the new woman by word and deed. While she had been raised and educated like her nineteenth-century female contemporaries to be reverent in church and obedient toward husbands, duly corsetted and diffident in speech, Elizabeth Cady Stanton defied all of those conventions. She walked alone. She suffered. She was there. On the occasion of the triumphal reception at her eightieth birthday party at the Metropolitan Opera House in 1895, she observed, "Having been accustomed for half a century to blame rather than praise, I was surprised with such a manifestation of approval" (Banner, 154).

Campbell describes the hero as "a personage of exceptional gifts. Frequently he is honored by his society, frequently unrecognized or disdained. . . . [T]ypically, the hero of the fairy tale achieves a domestic, microcosmic triumph, and the hero of myth a world-historical, macrocosmic triumph. . . . [T]he latter brings back from his adventure the means for the regeneration of his society as a whole" (37–38). The task is great, and it is subtle as well:

> If we could dredge up something forgotten not only by ourselves but by our whole generation or our entire civilization, we should indeed become the boon-bringer, the culture creator of our day — a personage of not only local but world historical moment. In a word: the first task of the hero is to retreat from the world scene of secondary effects to those casual zones of the psyche where the difficulties really reside, and there to clarify the difficulties, eradicate them in his own case (i.e., give battle to the nursery demons of his local culture) and break through. . . . (17–18)

For generations to come, Stanton redefined the psychological, legal, and political meaning of womanhood. She broke through the layers of acceptable female practice and stood her ground to question with original, heroic energy the men in her life, her church, and her country. She reached into the unconsciousness of society itself, rang the gong of the equality between men and women, and continued to ring it, sometimes in a total vacuum, to the chagrin of her father, her neighbors, and her nation, until she was dead. In this sense, she fragmented and finally helped to kill the social system as it was currently constituted in male hegemony. She began to think and dream a more just system to put in its place. It is a process in which many sensitized citizens are still actively engaged.

And just as Stanton "dredge[d] up something forgotten

not only by ourselves but by our whole generation or our entire civilization," Douglass dredged up the very fact of black personhood, in a hypocritical white nation that still condoned the enslavement of millions of black men, women, and children. In his role as a woman's rights man and by virtue of being probably the fiercest and most effective abolitionist and reformer of his time, Douglass, too, is a hero by Campbell's definition. He did not, like Elizabeth Cady Stanton, have to "retreat from the world scene of secondary effects to those casual zones of the psyche where the difficulties really reside," for he was already there. He was born into those zones as a slave. Together, with the struggles they personify, they represent the hope for the final evolution of American democracy.

Douglass emerged from the twilight zone of being black in the nineteenth century. His departure in Campbell's terms was embodied in his escape from slavery. According to Campbell, the pull of tradition operates like a tremendous negative magnet to any individual who contemplates the need to depart the status quo, and to be initiated into a moral framework beyond the limited confines of current social or political convention. Sometimes the need to depart from one's context is a freely made, conscious choice, but more often than not it is a matter of survival, with no way out but into risk-taking and expanded consciousness. In Douglass's case, it was not so much departure but genuine escape. In describing his thoughts and plans for escaping slavery in the 1830s, he observed:

> It is impossible for me to describe my feelings as the time of my contemplated start drew near. I had a number of warm-hearted friends in Baltimore, — friends that I loved almost as I did my life, — and the thought of being separated from them forever was painful beyond expression. It is my opinion that thousands would escape from slavery, who now remain, but for the strong cords of affection that bind them to their friends. The thought of leaving my friends was decidedly the most painful thought

with which I had to contend. The love of them was my tender
point, and shook my decision more than all things else. (*Narrative*, 110)

For Douglass, as for most of us, friendships and social ties
were so central as to overwhelm even the psychic necessity
of taking on a distinguishing, new idea or action, even if that
idea or action had to do with one's escape from human
bondage. Not only was the act of breaking free of his chains
terrifying for the fear of getting caught by unmerciful masters, but it also required the sacrifice of his friends.

Douglass did "depart" from slavery in September 1838,
and so began his development as an American hero. In
Campbell's terms, Douglass's arrival, or initiation, was
embedded in his self-taught education and expressed in muscular, moral outrage at the institution of slavery, the Christian church that condoned it, and the American society that
could not find courage enough to end it.

The return to face the community one originally departed
from confirms the hero's status, and Douglass literally
returned to Maryland, to some of the sites where he had been
enslaved, and talked to one of his aging former masters. On
another level, however, Douglass was in a perpetual state of
return as he contended continuously with the American society that had made slavery legal, continued to endorse it, and
also condoned the secondary status of women. He met with
his share of irate citizens who hated blacks or who were
totally inured to the institution of slavery and the second-
class status of women. In persistently reminding America of
its moral crime and demonstrating the healing power of his
own transformations, he was continually heroic.

As Campbell formulated it, the climax of the heroic function is to give birth to a new consciousness (16–17). It is in
departure from an intolerable present that the way to initiation into the personal unity of a new self, or even a new
nation, lies. The modern hero would have to embody and

enact a rediscovered unity between the conscious and the unconscious, between black and white, masculine and feminine. Douglass seems to have united such opposite elements in his own life. He married his moral sensitivity, usually considered a feminine attribute, with his marvelous power as a speaker, publicist, and lobbyist, traditionally considered masculine abilities. Similarly, Elizabeth Cady Stanton displayed the kind of powers of abstraction and visionary leadership theretofore thought to be the exclusive territory of men.

In the proximity of such birth is always a pall of resistance to the new, and the priests, ministers, and self-proclaimed upholders of current standards of virtue become the fiercest and cruelest resisters of an emerging ethos. So it is the protectors and guardians of custom who traditionally refuse to see the good in change, especially as it might represent their demise.

Stanton challenged the male priests of traditional society and annulled the laws of womanhood of her age. She gave birth by word and deed to new standards and expectations that would put the world on a new footing. Likewise, Douglass clearly subverted what was a justified practice of slavery and elevated the American consciousness to a new level. In effect, Stanton and Douglass presided over the dismemberment of the old and became midwives to the new. They threw nineteenth-century men and women back upon themselves, beckoning them to realize their full potential as human beings. These two heroes not only redrew the lineaments of God so that they would be equally expressed in the faces of men and women, blacks and whites (Campbell, 390), they thereby also changed the constitution of the American male soul. They hold within their giant examples the magic ceremony of initiatory male transformation.

Modern males are in a quandary about the sword. Douglass recasts the problem by showing us how to wield a moral sword. Similarly, Stanton carried in her ballot box the image of woman as political leader, change agent, and fully developed human being. Not only has she been an original, historic force behind the modern professional and political realization of women, but her example even today is enough to feminize men, for in so strengthening the feminine she has empowered its emergence in the male psyche. Just as Stanton at first whispered and diffidently demanded the vote for women, men must now require of themselves, at the altar of the Wesleyan Chapel, a voice for their uncorsetted, more loving, and more communicative selves.

The dynamics of the birth and development of the hero as conceived by Campbell and as personified by Frederick Douglass and Elizabeth Cady Stanton provide the principles by which white males can depart for Seneca Falls and navigate its dangerous precincts to arrive at their manhood. The process of such development is really just an enactment, on a dramatic and personal level, of the aboriginal rites of passage by which boys become men. If we can recognize that passage, then men, young men in particular, will depart increasingly for the new battlefront, the maze both within and without that leads to Seneca Falls, the site of the breakthrough, where the old self dies and is reborn, with Stanton and Douglass as the initiating elders.

In centering on Seneca Falls, I focus on a site that exists in actuality as well as in metaphor. Campbell writes:

> Wherever a hero has been born, has wrought, or has passed back into the void, the place is marked and sanctified. A temple is erected there to signify and inspire the miracle of perfect centeredness; for this is the place of the breakthrough into abundance. Someone at this point discovered eternity. The site can serve, therefore, as a support for fruitful meditation. Such temples are designed, as a rule, to simulate the four directions of the world horizon, the shrine or altar at the center being symbolical of the Inexhaustible Point. The one who enters the temple compound and proceeds to the sanctuary is imitating the deed of the original hero. His aim is to rehearse the universal pattern as a means of evoking within himself the recollection of the life-centering, life-renewing form. (43)

The original Wesleyan Chapel was, through the years, built over, patched, remodeled and almost totally obliterated. Happily, during the 1970s and 1980s, energetic townspeople assisted in establishing a Woman's Rights National Historic Park in Seneca Falls. The National Parks Service has now created a simple and dignified memorial to the First Woman's Rights Convention, with what remains of the Wesleyan Chapel at center. Two of its original walls and part of its roof have now been uncovered and preserved.

CHAPTER ELEVEN

The New Battlefield:
The Multiracial Children of Elizabeth Cady Stanton and Frederick Douglass

The minotaur that was slain in Seneca Falls in 1848 was the white American male himself, his racism and sexism. The way in and the way out again from that dangerous labyrinth that leads to the heart of modern America is to forge a path toward a new national community.

Once the decision is made to depart from the conventions of known society to seek our personhood, or once a wounding crisis propels us out (or in) to the uncharted territory where it lies buried, the geography of that search lies in the direction of what is most unknown, in the direction of the deepest, most difficult questions we have about ourselves and each other.

In considering the quality of men's lives, Sam Keen writes:

> To be on a quest is nothing more or less than to become an asker of questions. In the Grail legend, the classical tale of male heroicism, we are told that when the Knights of the Round Table set out on their quest, each one entered the forest at the place it was darkest and forged a path where none had been before. The inner, psychological meaning of this myth is that full manhood is to be found only when we commit ourselves to a life of questioning. (132)

The forest today is the human being, all of us. And to find ourselves, white males especially have to ask hard questions and explore in the hope of finding ourselves reflected back in the faces of women and people of color, those people personified by Stanton and Douglass. Manhood cannot be achieved in isolation. All of us are members of communities, and we have to learn to bring our quest out into the community, for all to be touched and challenged by it, the neighborhood, the nation, and the world.

It is vital for us to ride our horses into the forest of the unconscious, toward a kind of dark Wesleyan Chapel of the soul. And I do not have to be some psychoanalyst to know how to proceed. I know I would much rather ask the black man questions about those of his aspects which are most terrifying to me and find them true than to keep him enslaved in the closet of my unconscious, where he would otherwise remain a pent-up figure of terror. I would prefer to confirm that black men are more virile, more talented, and larger than life in all respects than to be terrified by their banging in the cellar of my private fears. It is probably obvious that when all is said and done, the near-obsession with black sexuality as it is carried down through countless white generations has to be primarily a shadow factor of the repressed sexuality of European Protestants and their legacy. The white male who has truly dived far down and caught the deep sea fish of his own phallus puts himself once and for all on a path of inner-directed personal development, no longer inclined to project the fear of his own inadequacies or sins or fantasies onto an enslaved group of others.

So one of my quests or questions as a white male and a seeker after manhood is to confront all the dehumanizing myths that white society imposes on blacks, including sexual ones, to ask questions of black thinkers, writers, and theorists, and to look with all intensity and honesty for a luminous circle that might cut across all color and gender boundaries. Likewise, I must take every opportunity to find not only a brother in the black man, but a sister in the woman. By admiring Elizabeth Cady Stanton, I commit myself to learning to appreciate the being of women, and to integrate my own feminine aspects. It is in discovering and honoring the feminine, in fact, that white American males first depart on the path. Through feeling, one is compelled to ask the necessary questions, difficult though they may be. Our questions are a response to the darkness, momentary explosions that light the way. Questions are the fallout of trying to love in this world.

If we men are not conversant with our own feelings, then we let women feel for us. And like it or not, women are the primary bearers of love and emotion in our culture, because men have allowed them to be. This frees the males to be men of unqualified action, powerful definers, supervisors, prepared to kill and be killed if necessary, free of the pedestrian cares and responsibility-producing virtues of feminine compassion and care. In this way, white males have become disembodied minds, abstract, inventive, intellectually skilled, soldierly.

Just as white males have, in effect, given over to black men their own deep and "dirty" sexual baggage, they have given to white women the realm of their sensitivity and compassion, the dark, viney growth of their tangled emotions. To regain their manhood, white males must reclaim the power to feel, and to take responsibility for their emotions.

To the extent that women and men have each evolved into nearly exclusive embodiments of femininity and masculinity respectively, women have been the uncontested representatives of the intuitive, relational aspects of being human. Women are less likely to spin off into a world of intellectual abstraction than are men. Women necessarily have to think more with their bodies within the realms of menstruation and childbirth, and thus have been considered more closely associated with the earth, as the repository of cycles and rhythms. Women seem wiser in a real, flesh and blood way, for living closer to the fonts of birth and death, blood and milk. Women have the dignity of moving in the rhythm of tides and seasons, and their intelligence emerges more organically out of the bone and flesh. They have more to do with survival than war, and are closer to loving than killing. Feminine power is associated with seeing between the abstract lines and angles that all-male men tend to draw. Femaleness has resided in relationships and community as opposed to the alone-male, battling silently and apart.

The female is softer, more magical than the male. The male is more obvious, more overt, more outer-directed, as suggested by his penis, which hangs on the outside. The woman is more hidden, more between the lines, more like the vagina, a complex, folded flower harbored inside. How real are these separate attributes? For no male is exclusively rough and tough, and no female is merely soft and intuitive. All of us have qualities of both male and female, and in the light of the mythic events of Seneca Falls, we must attempt to balance and integrate our various aspects. If we fail to do so, it is at our peril.

The white male has tended to become the superhuman mind, a technological genius, the imposer of designs and plans and shopping malls on mother earth. Aside from the truth that this kind of genius has created technological miracles that have quickened civilization in remarkable ways, it is also true that the world community is suffering immensely from the by-products of this abstraction: pollution and the perpetual menace of sophisticated warfare as a result of this almost exclusive life of the mind, which is lived to the detriment of the more feminine aspects.

The lost feminine aspect of men is that wilderness that cartographers and technological geniuses have tried to exorcise with the machinery of compass and calculator. It is the scented and dark content of the perfectly drawn square. For men to regain their wholeness, they must depart momentarily from the exclusive and often arrogant life of their rational minds, dive down into the feminine and relational aspects of being human, and open its energy flow once again. Under ideal circumstances, the fully realized man, the kind of hero we search to be here, lets the mighty feminine energy flow up into his mind from down below. The tools, or weapons, for awakening the renounced feminine are precisely the questions of our horrific times, the questions of patriotism and materialism, of racism and sexism, of individuality and community, of love and heroism.

For her part, the female has tended to bypass the glaring light of the potentially killing mind, and to live rather one-sidedly in a neighborhood of exclusive emotions that undergo little rational scrutiny and obey no laws nor take on obvious, rational shape. Women need to open the life force of the mind, unhindered by male control, and to discover for themselves its ancient, knifelike power.

To the degree that his latent feminine is allowed to flare up, inform and permeate the fullest architecture of himself, the male gains true, personal power. The female, likewise, gains her utmost power to the degree that the knifelike masculine aspect is allowed to descend into her being and do its work of defining, separating, and penetrating there, to be immersed in milk. To the degree that each of us maintains some dialogue with the male and female aspects within, and succeeds in achieving some sense of balance with regard to the cross-fire of the up and down, and in and out of life energy, then the full potential of individually evolving human beings within a common circle of humanity can be realized.

Instead of men being expected merely to carry weapons and to prepare for physical violence, and women being expected to support his strivings and to keep the home fires burning, the examples of Elizabeth Cady Stanton and Frederick Douglass suggest that both men and women can become relentless, fierce fighters after justice, first by over-throwing and radicalizing their own exclusively masculine and feminine elements, and then by carrying the spirit of Seneca Falls to all points. Together men and women, the combatants in such new wars, who have been initiated by the events of Seneca Falls, will help even to redefine war itself, its enemies, its objectives. For to the extent that our own pysches do become the real battlefields, and we recognize ourselves to be the enemy, power will be redefined and war as an institution will cease to exist. The creative tension between different aspects of ourselves and between different points of view, as expressed politically, spiritually, and artistically in a community of individuals, will eventually provide a basis on which to make bloodless war within the human family in a perpetual attempt to come to terms with each other. We need to set forth into the forests of all that we do not know about each other.

It is in the act of questioning, or questing, that we find ourselves stumbling toward Seneca Falls. Otherwise we begin to spin dangerous, isolating, and violence-producing cocoons about ourselves. We need constant departures and the crises of perpetual woundings and the danger of lonely and difficult journeys as a context in which to grow as men. Actual soldiers of any nation are just as much children to women and mothers as they are potential usurpers and killers to men and fathers. After Seneca Falls, war becomes the struggle to lay claim as peacefully as possible to the just and righteous territory of human rights, access to education, respect for the environment, and, central to all of these, equality and unity among the races and between the sexes.

The feminist theorist Robin Morgan quotes Hannah Arendt in *On Violence:* "The chief reason warfare is still with us is neither a secret death wish of the human species, nor an irrepressible instinct of aggression . . . but the simple fact that no substitute for this final arbiter in international affairs has yet appeared on the political scene" (quoted in Morgan, 1). Morgan goes on to observe:

> That substitute has now appeared. As with every major shift in human history, it manifests itself at first almost naively, from an unexpected (even ridiculed) direction. Only after such a shift has demonstrated its energy as a transformative force does it seem obvious and inevitable. . . . That substitute — that transformative force . . . is women and women's culture as a global influence. (1)

To the degree that individual power cliques, whether they be nations, coteries of white males, or the fraternity of arms merchants, are actively scrutinized by spiritually balanced women and men baptized by the events of Seneca Falls, the mode of problem-solving will take the form of an intimate family decision, not the abstracted, anonymous endgames of a bloody battlefield. According to a new definition of manhood and womanhood, inter-country disputes will increasingly tend to be solved by argument, mediation, and unified economic action (Miller, "Battlefield Visit," 29).

By listening to their own feminine mutterings, men can choose to become revolutionary minutemen for the cause of personal and societal transformation, against the old nation-states of prejudice, repression, and brute power. This axis of revolutionary-mindedness, which governs and replicates the flow of life energy itself, begins with the feminine and cuts right through the heart of any value system that vaunts the superiority of one race or sex over another. Men are called by the events of Seneca Falls to ground themselves in the simple values of fairness and love, and then to be poised to meet social and political experience with a discerning, radical soul-sword. By this process, all of us become the multiracial children of Elizabeth Cady Stanton and Frederick Douglass, men and women of every economic level, of every national origin, global citizens, patriots and matriots of America and of the world.

Keen adds a spiritual dimension:

The question Christianity, as well as every religious tradition, puts to men and women yesterday and today is: Do I find my fulfillment in asserting my will to power over myself and others, or in surrendering to myself and others in a spirit of empathy and compassion? And if I can only be myself by surrendering, to what, to whom do I surrender? (102–103)

He answers his own question:

We may liberate a single insight about manhood that continues to be as revolutionary as it was two millennia ago. A man finds fulfillment (spiritual and sexual) only when he turns aside from willfulness and surrenders to something beyond self. Virility involves life in communion. When we try to discover the principle of manhood within the isolated self, we will end up not fulfilling the self but destroying it. Manhood can be defined only in relational terms. How large and generous we may become depends on the size of the Other we take into ourselves. (102)

The spiritual intensity that animated the lives and work of Mother Stanton and Father Douglass exemplifies the revolutionary American and democratic vision to which men might submit and pledge their loyalty, in order to earn their manhood and their lover's stripes for the next hundreds of years. These figures invite men to submit specifically to a moral, God-rooted universe which they know intuitively to be operating, vouchsafed by natural law. The manhood of those white males who understand and succeed in integrating their masculine and feminine aspects will become "large and generous" accordingly. The radical events of Seneca Falls are an invitation to heed the call to arms in a new kind of war, to participate in a new mass, a sacred ceremony of love and reconciliation among races and sexes, and as we shall see, within the ecological web of the earth as well.

~~~~~

CHAPTER TWELVE

A Map for the Forever Young

Consider teenagers, who frequently do not hold a map to their own personal power, let alone a moral map to and from Seneca Falls. I have counselled them for ten years. The essential rebelliousness of modern teenagers is an expression of an urgent longing for initiation into a greater social myth that now no longer exists in an obvious, cultural way. Like spiders trailing silk threads in sunlight, they are flailing about blindly in the hope of catching something that feels as good and powerful as sex or rock and roll, something transcendent that might explain the infinity of time and the terror of love and loneliness.

And it is not only teenagers who consciously and unconsciously search for a spiritual direction or an initiation story. It is almost everyone. Underneath every business suit, behind every beautiful face, in the haunted dreams of old men and women, and under the surprised faces of exquisitely self-conscious teenagers, there is the buzzing of something beyond, something just out of reach that, if acquired, would somehow explain who we are.

Referring to women's need to think and act independently, Elizabeth Cady Stanton said in her "Solitude of Self" speech in 1892:

> They must know something of the laws of navigation. To guide our own craft, we must be captain, pilot, engineer, with chart and compass to stand at the wheel; to watch the winds and waves, and know when to take in the sail, and to read the signs in the firmament over all. It all matters not whether the solitary voyager is man or woman; nature, having endowed them

equally, leaves them to their own skill and judgement in the hour of danger, and, if not equal to the occasion, alike they perish. (248)

It used to be the priests and ministers who held the map. Now it is the psychologist who purports to know the laws of navigation and to hold the compass for intellectual and spiritual development. But as a man from Seneca Falls, I here lay out a chart of departure, arrival, and return that fits into one's back pocket. It includes a brief psychology of being young, restless, and lost. The essential self-development process is hardly discussed in schools or religious study classes, rarely talked about at home, encountered only faintly in readings in English class, touched on only slightly in therapy work.

The process of growing up in America during the teenage years is fundamentally about departures, about breaking away from the ostensible hold of parents and the status quo that does not acknowledge a crazy and beautiful way out. For adolescents, most adults are tired out or angry most of the time. Their breath smells, some of them drive cars like Plymouths and Chevrolets — "cars like that." For many such reasons, they are not often regarded as allies by teenagers. In all, adults are alien creatures and the appropriate emotion to be expressed toward them is either to pity or to fear them, or simply to shut down one's expectations, responses, and dreams in relation to them.

For young people, adults have given in to the distress of being alive and have chosen the old people's path of least resistance. And that's where they hunker down, away from the immediacy of the moment, away from the crisis that love provokes, far and away from sensual evenings, the sound of rain, and the fingers of fog that grasp January trees, evoking memory and dream. Grown-ups desensitize themselves, hide behind their wrinkles, behind their ties, their glasses, and their complacency, behind talk of weather, sports, and world news. Adults are hidden in their depreciating bodies, buffered by the authority of age, lost to the kiss, removed from the electricity of spring, and unacquainted with the terror of not being accepted by one's peers.

Adults look unhappy, act uninspired, and can be so easily fooled it isn't funny. Grown-ups seem to reach a certain point in their lives, perhaps at a particular age, or job seniority, or family size, at which time they become just like their own parents, and lose the battle to remain forever young. They lose their ideals, their sense of moral authority. They grow up and give in to the way things are done in the world. Money, the right friends, the perfect vacations, all take dominance over the nuances and subtleties of being alive and bringing in the soul-sheaves of love, joy, and enthusiasm.

While we are young, anything is possible. The horizon of fulfillment for every teenager stretches out as far as the eye can see. Television and movies invite everyone to reach for the star of material and personal success. And within the teenage heart of almost every boy and girl is the passionate wish, impossible to disprove for at least another twenty years, that success is imminent, that it is just a matter of time.

The high school years are a breeding ground for the dream of succeeding at all levels, sexually, socially, intellectually, athletically, and professionally. There are relatively no limits, no reasons not to go all the way, to the right college, the right job, the right address. And the voice of one's compassionate nature, the private rapture in response to sunsets, the cherished wish that one will be completely cradled and understood by another human being, all remain as torches to one's movement forward into the dark, limitless world. This is the human spirit blazing forth, the tender, wily, and crazy aspects of being a human being, especially a young one. There is a certain fragrance of crushed violets in the mind of every teenager.

Like dogs sniffing the wind, teenagers follow a curlicue of rapturous perfume that threads its way into relationships, classrooms, playing fields, into driving cars, playing rock and roll, and on into the future of the world and across the brow of all that suffers today but won't tomorrow. For teenagers, immortality comes walking in big gaudy boots and kicks up its crazy heels in every room in the house.

When one's mind is still pickled in hormones, and physical health is the currency by which most of life is spent, there is no wonder that the pragmatic, the commitment to work, the ability to plan and anticipate all surrender to teenage desire to kiss and couple with the moon. And so the fireball of blind sexual energy streaks across the sky, and intellectual knives rattle in their scabbards, while a sort of terribly awkward moose of spiritual loneliness and gawkishness wanders through the underbrush of life, screaming silently for a magic spell to change one into an eagle or a brilliant flame or even just a mechanical pencil to be put away anonymously in a pocket.

While the teenage engines, physical, emotional, and intellectual, are firing like a new car, the kid at the wheel hasn't fully learned to drive, doesn't really know the laws of navigation, doesn't altogether understand who he or she is, and is all the while making the car swerve at full speed from one side of the road to the other. This crazy driver is precisely the uncoordinated soul of every teenager that is madly trying to make sense out of it all and can't be expected in a million years to know how the whole thing works. Teenagers carry into the family, neighborhood, and school a truckload of flowers, notions, truth, junk, attitudes, friendships, and unasked and as yet unanswered questions and dump it all right in front of serious, status quo adults.

In the face of teenage children, grown-ups have to scramble for answers, rethink their very lives. Some grown-ups feel so stressed and challenged by the surprise of teenagers that they have to lie to survive, or, because of the freshness and originality of the reality that teenagers represent, have to seriously reexamine the very foundations and institutions upon which they have built their own lives.

Some adults retain credibility in the face of the upheaval inherent in being a teenager, and succeed in maintaining a position of influence in the lives of young people. But most adults fail the test of credibility as applied by these perceptive, zealous, and ardent kids who can detect an old person from miles away.

But what happens, unfortunately, is that while teenagers seem to have the godlike energy of self-transformation by which to change themselves and the world, they do not actually depart on their requisite quests. Over a period of time they turn themselves inside out to become just like their own parents, with the very same fears, prejudices, and hesitations. The heart they once wore on their sleeve is exchanged for the cool, rational disposition of adulthood, or what passes for adulthood. For the horizon of infinite possibilities that the teenager sees is substituted a box of sorts, a set of constraints and conventions of wallet, work, and worry. The adult world doesn't seem to accommodate infinity or dream or love very well. This life is more about endings, tragedies, disappointments, war, and the finite clashing of two or more irreconcilable points of view, not their confluence and coordination into a unity of being.

Most adults are more comfortable with "no" than with "yes," more knowledgeable about walls than horizons. And so the transformation of the fire of the teenage heart into the ice of the adult mind is almost inevitable. What else is there to do but to grow up, leave off doing childish things, and assume responsibility for one's self and family and community? Boys and girls become men and women. And the cycles of birth, youth, adulthood, and death revolve like a square wheel, without the spiritual aids of symbol, myth, and rites of passage that would carry one to a true personhood.

So the spirituality of being a teenager is usually left behind along with baseball cards, leggos, and knock-knock jokes where, for most of us, it twitches, occasionally cries out in pain, and eventually dies for lack of respect.

Adults are left without spiritual maps for the pursuit of balance between mind and heart, of vision toward the entire planet. We are left rudderless, lost in the dark, navigating by the seat of our pants. And, unfortunately, into the vacuum left by the stuff of spirituality that could once vibrate to rock and roll and revolve like a personal moon inside our souls, all too frequently goes alcohol, drugs, and ambitions for money and power over others. So boys and girls become pained, uninitiated men and women. Once the red cabbages and eagle feathers of the soul are bartered away, there is never an adequate substitute. The rest of one's life is spent searching for something to take its place, and crashing into the walls in which we have chosen to imprison ourselves. And the pathology of longing for the wrong things is the substance of modern psychology (Miller, "Adults Search for the Teenage Spirituality Left Behind," 26).

Youth's excess and unchannelled energy is essentially enthusiasm without a metaphor, perfume without a bottle, a landscape without a map. Without map or metaphor, this marvelous spray of being alive finally dies down. It has no way of organizing itself, of being disciplined by a governing idea, and therefore does not gain force and longevity. Whereas water forced through a fountain gains power and form, water that just bubbles up from the ground soon dissipates and is re-absorbed.

The political and spiritual conjunction of a white woman and a black man in Seneca Falls in 1848 describes the dynamic rite of departure, arrival, or initiation, and return by which boys and girls can draw on their underground spiritual power and rise to the occasion of becoming men and women in the modern sense. The initiatory drama enacted by Stanton and Douglass personifies a coming of age ceremony, both individually and socially, in America. By stepping into the moral and magic circle that the actions of these two heroes define, young people in particular can find their path of adulthood while retaining their mad, crushed-violets energy.

How can we define a possible point of departure for young men and women as they might journey toward an understanding of Seneca Falls? Where is the Wesleyan Chapel?

Even in these difficult times of blurred moral boundaries, young people are still raised with some semblance of moral and spiritual awareness. It may happen at Sunday school or synagogue or at summer camp or at the knees of parents. But the relatively sacred matters of telling the truth, cooperating, and being patient and compassionate remain alive in the value systems of American institutions. "Relatively sacred" because increasingly less allegiance is paid to these values, perhaps since the advent of the Industrial Revolution and the ascendancy of time and money. Traditional spiritual virtues such as compassion and love and patience are clearly less stringently taught and enforced in human communities in America, and they are less and less understood as involving spiritual laws that carry dread consequences if violated.

As one result, when teenagers are asked in countless ways either to distinguish themselves from their peers by having an opinion that rests on solid moral ground or to do what most of us do, which is to hedge and hide in the shadows of anonymity, most young people choose to live in the shadows. It is downright difficult to separate oneself, as Elizabeth Cady Stanton and Frederick Douglass each did, as all heroes have done, from the comfort of convention and tradition, to destroy in order that one may create. The process of stepping forth from the mass of individuals to stand on firm spiritual ground is terrifying, usually leaving one alone and vulnerable, with no visible means of support.

Luckily for those young people who are even contemplating taking a moral stand based on any form of spiritual principle, it just so happens in the process of individuating that the spiritual principle or set of principles by which one acts in this sense somehow has a mysterious life of its own in the depths of the universe. Spiritual laws and moral codes have their roots invariably in the Great Spirit, in God, as it is expressed by one religion or another and by all indigenous peoples in all parts of the world. And, therefore, God, on this metaphor/map of Seneca Falls, must be clearly marked, not in terms of any particular religious tradition but as the ultimate energy source toward which we are continuously, spontaneously, and sometimes inexplicably drawn, as a landmark in our comings and goings.

But high and mighty concepts of moral or spiritual principle are themselves hugely vulnerable to the charge that they are simply expressions of a paternalistic church, of male exponents applying abstract dictums to a passive congregation. Luckily for our purposes, the spiritual stuff from which such laws and codes are originally extracted, is very much the essential content of what traditionally has been considered the attributes of the feminine: that is, the instinct to love rather than to overpower; the responsibility to nurture rather than to compete; the relational abilities to empathize and show compassion. All find their counterparts at the core of universal spiritual teachings. Perhaps women, as the ancient force behind the establishment of agriculture, embody the fundamental matrix of the rules of community which, at heart or beneath the level of convention, are necessarily and mysteriously spiritual. And in this sense, for white males to depart on journeys toward their own manhood, they must begin in feeling. To get at the rightness of things, at justice, at the proper symmetry of human relationships within a family or a nation, or within themselves, they must begin on female ground. Here, then, is that luminous first step: to become a feeling human male.

Because there is a decided lack of vigorous effort to help young people make moral maps by which to find themselves and progress according to some guiding, humane standard, young people's development is marked by tremendous pitfalls and dangerous mountain paths. The holes that the absence of a direct, personal development philosophy leaves in the lives of most teenagers, let alone most human beings, can be filled in a variety of ways, and they are. Because young people have a natural capacity, even a need, to feel high, in the absence of clear guidelines to help them learn how to feel gratified by living wisely and courageously and judiciously, drugs and alcohol substitute to imitate the feeling of empowerment. Thousands upon thousands of young people — and adults — simply spin off into the darkness artificially lit by alcohol and drugs, where their own spiritual and intellectual lights finally dim. Those who return are still all too few.

Music is also used to provide scripts or mini-maps of survival for young people. The lyrics of rock and roll, rap, and the blues all go a long way in offering a vocabulary for the struggle to discover the furthermost high and low limits of what it means to be a human being, to destroy present circumstances by the power of sheer decibels and then to recreate the world with musical art. Hard rock dissonance is a lingua franca for the destructive-creative impulse inherent in teenagers' defiant need to depart in particular from the hold of their parents and various authority figures, a kind of dress rehearsal for the opportunity to get sleek for the long haul of life itself, and even to change the world.

To try too hard to clarify the half-dark, half-ungovernable hormonal music of being a teenager is, probably, a stupid and even impossible enterprise. Maybe its duality of creativeness and destructiveness is meant to be entirely indecipherable, totally confusing to those who are experiencing it both as teenagers and as parents. But we know that in the construct of adolescence, whatever smacks of the status quo has to be questioned, even destroyed, or at least intellectually or emotionally torn down, opened up, looked over and under for a better way, and, if necessary, disposed of entirely. This teenage process of destruction of the found world is essentially creative, because it necessarily leads to new approaches, unlikely combinations, and mistakes that often tend to be right on, and eventually results in the formation of character and personality. In this way the journey from youth to adulthood clearly parallels the need of the hero or the self-actualizing individual to step free from the society as it presently is and to arrive at a new vision that superannuates it. The reticence of teenagers, the flippancy, the code words for a secret life are all metaphors for their enthusiastic attempt at snubbing the adult world, departing from it, and searching for a new horizon. But without a map, the journey is not made, the ceremony ignored.

CHAPTER THIRTEEN

Sermon from the Wesleyan Chapel:
The New Landscape

According to Alvin Toffler, civilization is reeling from the
Third Wave breaking upon its informational, technological, and political systems, "tearing our families apart, rock-
ing our economy . . . shattering our values" (26). *The Third
Wave* defines the cultural antecedents of the First and Second Waves, that is, the Agricultural and Industrial Revolutions respectively, and then documents the emergence of a
global revolution in thought and relationships. Toffler writes:

> Humanity faces a quantum leap forward. It faces the deepest
> social upheaval and creative restructuring of all time. Without
> clearly recognizing it, we are engaged in building a remarkable
> new civilization from the ground up. This is the meaning of the
> Third Wave. (26)

Besides war, poverty, lack of renewable energy, and political systems inadequate to the needs of the Third Wave, Toffler lists "ecological degradation" as one of the world's most
pressing problems. Written well before the breakup of the
Soviet Union, the tragedy of the Valdez oil spill, or the piti-
ful attempts of the United Nations as world peace keeper,
Toffler says that what is especially required is the creation of
global systems that manage the breakdown of old, industrial
values and supply new lines of loyalty and vision that will
sufficiently reposition white males, or as he calls them,
"endangered elites," and nurture "a radical expansion of
political participation" (452).

The Agricultural Revolution emerged about 8,000 years ago when animals were first domesticated, when land was first owned and permanent settlements established. At that time, the trades and arts developed, as did a ruling class, and the idea of material wealth was born. The agriculturists were able to produce more food per acre than the previous hunters and gatherers but it was of poorer quality. At the same time, as a people who were now anchored to a piece of land, these first agriculturists became more vulnerable to invasion and oppression. They were also the first victims of environmental mishandling, as they could not move away from their own wastes.

As the Agricultural Revolution was a response to wildlife scarcity, the Industrial Revolution, or Second Revolution, was a response to energy and land scarcity. Manual work became harder and more repetitive, and the cities became filthy. But it was the thought revolution produced by the Industrial Revolution that was most significant. Men then began to think in terms of profit, and of the earth as mere raw material. In the name of profit both labor and resources were treated with cold indifference.

Now a Third Revolution is dawning. Environmentalist Donella H. Meadows observes:

> Few of us picking up trash and carrying Earth banners are thinking of a thoroughgoing revision of human culture. But down deep most of us know that's the direction our concern will lead. We know it is impossible to go on finding and wasting oil, leveling forests, paving land, dumping poisons, and multiplying our numbers. A new way of life, a new set of thoughts must be found. . . . [A Third Revolution] will change the face of the land and human institutions, hierarchies, self-definitions, and cultures. It will take centuries.

Luckily, the wanton consumption of earth and air for profit and the poisonous wastes that are the by-products of blind greed have finally produced a mature, worldwide environmental movement. Once only the environmentalist and the cloistered researcher preached the green religion of the future and prophesied disaster in the dwindling number of least terns and snail darters. Now everyone is talking about the imperatives of the environment. We finally understand that if the rivers evaporate or the forests disappear or the soil becomes poisoned, then cities and civilizations come apart. Unless we take care of our mud, our breezes, our surf, and our stones, we die.

Certainly, national and international environmental legislation is fundamental to the protection of air, water, and land. Enforcement of firm environmental standards and the intelligent local community efforts of zoning boards and conservation commissions can provide the necessary infrastructure of a healthy planet. But any attempt to work respectfully and cooperatively with the earth is itself doomed if it is merely a legislative movement that proscribes behavior and enforces penalties, as necessary as these are, and does not embark on the real and revolutionary process of making fundamental changes in the ways we love, hate, solve problems, and do business on this planet.

Ensuring a healthy planet has to be accomplished in terms of the landscape of our characters. It is upon the ground of our collective value system that the earth will ultimately be lost or regained. To hold the most potent ecological vision is first to draw in the earth's dust an outline of a human being, and to include the poetry, the love, fear, and courage of which human beings are capable. Then we need to draw these same human lines to include rivers, mountains, trees, and oceans so that the territory of being human includes these living things as well.

The Third Revolution, or Third Wave, is implicit in the events and players of Seneca Falls. The industrial machine in the hands of white men has become the implement of our own destruction. We must understand that part of successfully realizing oneself is to transform the way we treat the earth, its air and water. To treat the earth henceforward in a more intelligent and embracing manner requires that we redefine the values upon which industrial nations have built their wealth. The earth is just the mud tablet on which we tell the story of who we are. If we kill each other or if we dirty the air or sully the rivers and oceans, then the story is written in blood and poison (Miller, "Defining Ourselves," 22).

Men's remarkable technological skill in developing weapons of war is a function of remarkably intelligent endeavor performed on a shifting grid of warring tribes, clans, and nation states. It is probably the paramount manifestation of male inventiveness and the most poignant symbol of men's cruel destructiveness toward their own kind and the planet they call home. The jet engine, the nuclear reactor, the polio vaccine, or literally any of the technological miracles of the last fifty years that either heal or kill, all demonstrate that the scientist is next to God in power. But the exclusive, abstract power of men has reached the threshold of mass self-destruction, and society needs the influence of the feminine in men, as well as women, in the labs and the pentagons of the world to heal this planet. It is obvious that the blind ambition after pure profit, and the largely unregulated application of white-male-directed technology, is responsible for the environmental malady in which we find ourselves. And having reached a threshold of what is a corrupt technological return, men are floundering for those missing feminine qualities with which to inform the use of that technology and to ensure that its future applications are more cooperative and nurturing.

Sam Keen observes:

> What some feminists now disparagingly refer to as "patriarchal technology" has given us a godlike capacity to shape matter and fulfill our dreams. But it has brought its opposite demonic attribute — the ability to destroy life. Millennia before the steam engine, the Greeks noticed that anything carried to excess bears the seeds of its own destruction. Within our century, the spiritual triumph of science and technology has gradually become our nemesis. Our increasing industrial pollution is

only the latest version of the vultures that eat the liver of Prometheus as he is chained to the rock of his hubris. . . . At the moment of our apotheosis, we are being humiliated by our creations. Our machines have turned against us. As weapons and pollution threaten our existence we approach an era in which the practice of science and technology, which has been the dominant source of masculine pride for nearly two centuries, must give way to some new vocation, some new mode of masculine identity. (105–106)

In 1848, the same year as the First Woman's Rights Convention, a major water pump company was founded in Seneca Falls. Goulds Pumps would go on to be a one-product multimillion dollar company that today exports its technologically advanced wares the world over. Paradoxically, the rise of the Industrial Revolution and the ascendancy of the machine also provided ground for the cause of women's rights to become ascendant. Formerly, in an agrarian society, the men were at home to rule the roost and remain in charge of the traditional social fabric. When men began to leave home for twelve hours at the factory, women necessarily had to assume a more prominent role as active agents in the affairs of the family and community.

Angela Davis, on the other hand, theorizes that women became trapped in a "domestic void" as the Industrial Revolution usurped the manufacture of goods for which they formerly had been responsible at home (129), since women had traditionally made soap, candles, clothing, and so forth. Speaking of white women, she writes: "When manufacturing moved out of the home and into the factory, the ideology of womanhood began to raise the wife and mother as ideals. . . . [A]s wives, they were destined to become appendages to their men" (32).

While men gained in their ascendancy in the realm of technology, women naturally became tinkerers and then veritable inventors in the machinery of their own empowerment. Because of limited access to education, and the constraints imposed on them by church and state, women have used the last century and a half to discover their more determinant, more masculine selves outside of the home.

Just as men will have to break into the reality of the feminine and abscond with a North Star orientation that moves them closer to love and cooperative values, so women, as with the ancient male Prometheus, will have to be thieves and outlaws in order to break into the vaults of highly specialized, technical mastery. Some women have been able to begin this work, but only when the technology of the masculine mind is completely drenched with the feeling-feminine will the power of technology truly be able to change the world, and help to realign it on an axis of moral balance and ecological unity. Men whose feminine and masculine components are sufficiently realized and made fierce by the ionizing events of Seneca Falls can consciously promulgate the Third Revolution. As they succeed in coordinating their own souls around more equal elements of both, the new world of a healed, physical planet will follow.

The gong of the consciousness of a Third Revolution was rung in Seneca Falls, and we can use its power to dedicate ourselves to the spiritualization of business and commerce. Such a green church would have to offer a new covenant between human beings and planet Earth, at the altar of which is inscribed a code of values in which love for each other and humility toward the earth is carved in stone. The old Wesleyan Chapel in Seneca Falls in which Elizabeth Cady Stanton and Frederick Douglass in effect said mass for a new social, political, and spiritual world can be a prototype of that temple of human consciousness in which air, water, and fire have a place in the congregation.

The reform movements of the nineteenth century had no overt consciousness of the ecological systems of the planet. It is intriguing to note, however, that Frederick Douglass, after witnessing the furor that the Seneca Falls Convention had caused in the press, observed that a convention to discuss the rights of animals would not have caused more commotion than this convention for women's rights. And in her convention speech Elizabeth Cady Stanton referred, in a kind of green mysticism, to "this beautiful earth" as the home of both men and women equally. (The extensive gardens and orchards of her Seneca Falls Washington Street home would suggest that she was indeed involved in the rhythms of the seasons and had fragrant dirt beneath her fingernails.)

Along with the other metaphors Seneca Falls carries for us here, it is significant that its site was also the center of the Six Nations of the Iroquois, a people, like all indigenous peoples of this continent, whose intelligence was grounded in ecological relationships, the consciousness of which was lost at the hands of the Industrial Revolution. Their long houses, their tools, their metaphors, all drew from a natural landscape that unites man, tree, water, and woman in a mythic unity. Stanton's knowledge of the esteemed position of women in Iroquois society certainly argues for the presence of Native Americans in the green congregation of the Third Revolution.

Stanton openly admired the historic role of Iroquois women, who owned property, were politically influential, and were primary in motherhood in the democratic, Iroquois polity that was all but in shreds at the time of the convention. She spoke specifically of Iroquois women in an 1891 speech before the National Council of Women, drawing from the memoirs of an upstate missionary:

> Usually the females ruled the house. The stores were in common; but woe to the luckless husband or lover who was too shiftless to do his share of the providing. No matter how many children, or whatever goods he might have in the house, he might at any time be ordered to pick up his blanket and budge; and after such an order it would not be healthful for him to attempt to disobey. The house would be too hot for him . . . unless saved by the intercession of some aunt or grandmother. . . . The women were the great power among the clan, as everywhere else. They did not hesitate, when occasion required, "to knock off the horns [sic], as it was technically called, from the head of a chief and send him back to the ranks of the warriors.

The original nomination of the chiefs also always rested with the women. (quoted in Wagner, "The Iroquois Confederacy," 218–19)

Matilda Joslyn Gage, a colleague of Stanton and Anthony's and a co-author with them in the *History of Woman Suffrage,* wrote extensively about the Iroquois, or Haudenosaunee — the People of the Long House. In the 1870s, as President of the National Woman Suffrage Association, she came out with a series of articles featured in the *New York Evening Post.* Sally Roesch Wagner's recent research tells us that Stanton and Gage "became increasingly disenchanted with the inability/unwillingness of Western institutions to change and embrace the liberty of not just women, but all disenfranchised groups. They looked elsewhere for their vision of the 'regenerated world'" which they both predicted. "And they found it — right next door . . . a cosmological world-view which they believed to be far superior to the patriarchal one of the white nation in which they lived" ("The Root of Oppression," 224).

Wagner writes that the "virtual absence of rape by Indian men, commented upon by many eighteenth and nineteenth century Indians [sic] and non-Indians [sic] reporters alike, was a behavior difficult to comprehend in a European tradition which legalized both marital rape and wife beating." Alice Fletcher, suffragist and ethnographer of the time, spoke in 1888 of the right of Indian women to own property which they brought into marriage, at the International Council of Women, which Stanton and Anthony both attended (225).

Iroquois women had their own chiefs and a judiciary which Gage called the Council of Matrons. Wagner cites an instance in which Iroquois women addressed the last general council held by the United States with the Confederacy at Canandaigua in 1794:

Iroquois women countered a prayer offered by Jemima Wilkinson, the itinerant preacher, who called on the Indians to repent. The Iroquois women responded through their representative that "the white people had pressed and squeezed them together, until it gave them great pain at their hearts, and they thought the white people ought to give back all the lands they had taken from them." They, in turn, called on the white people to "repent and wrong the Indians no more." (220)

It is the ghostly Iroquois feminine, the "transformative force" of women in Robin Morgan's words, to which we men must now learn to pay attention if we are to evolve a consciousness of the unity of life and accomplish a Third Revolution. The text of such relationship-consciousness might be the speech ascribed to the Duwamish Chief Seattle, said to have been spoken at Elliot Bay in December 1854 in response to a U.S offer to buy native lands in what is now Washington State. The words of Chief Seattle have undergone alterations, until heavily rewritten by a screenwriter in the early 1970s. The fictionalized version has had wide circulation recently and is often delivered at Earth Day ceremonies. That version appears in Appendix 5.

Chief Seattle's actual words, spoken in the Salish dialect (Egan), were indeed delivered during his 1854 meeting with U.S. Indian Superintendent Isaac Stevens, in response to Washington's request to buy his people's land. The Chief's words were first published in English in 1887, by Seattle's translator, Dr. Henry A. Smith. The speech, as recollected by Smith, suffers from a quasi-poetical Victorian prose style which must surely detract from the Chief's primal intentions on that day. Spoken by this human casualty of the westward movement in America, the speech calls the bluff of President Franklin Pierce's good wishes, and prophesies a kind of human ecological justice in America[1]:

1 Smith described Chief Seattle for the *Seattle Sunday Star* (October 29, 1877) "as noble as that of the most civilized military chieftain in command of the forces of a continent. Neither his eloquence, his dignity, nor grace was acquired. They were as native to his manhood as leaves and blossoms to a flowering almond.

His influence was marvelous. He might have been an emperor but all his instinct was democratic, and he ruled his subjects with kindness and paternal benighty." (Anderson, 383)

Yonder sky has wept tears of compassion on my people for centuries untold. To us it appears changeless and eternal. Yet it may change. Today is fair. Tomorrow may be overcast with clouds. My words are like the stars that never change. Whatever I say the Great Chief at Washington can rely on as certainly as he can upon the return of the seasons.

This white chief[2] says: Big Chief at Washington sends us greetings of friendship and goodwill. That is kind of him, for we know he has little need of our friendship in return. His people are many. They are like grass that covers the vast prairies!

My people are few. They resemble the scattering trees of a storm-swept plain.

The great, and I presume good, White Chief sends us word that he wishes to buy our lands but is willing to allow us enough to live comfortably. That indeed appears just, even generous.

For the red man no longer has rights that the White Chief need respect. His offer may be wise, too, as we no longer need extensive country.

Once our people covered the land as waves of a wind-ruffled sea cover its shell-paved floor. That time has long since passed away, with the greatness of tribes that are now but a mournful memory.

I will not dwell on, nor mourn over, our untimely decay, nor reproach my paleface brothers with hastening it. We, too, may have been to blame.

Youth is impulsive. When our young men grow angry at some real or imaginary wrong, and disfigure their faces with

---

This quotation and the text of the speech are taken verbatim from a book written by Eva Anderson, entitled *Chief Seattle* (pp.383, 204-211). However, where her text uses an Indian word, "tyee," for chief, I use "chief." Although her book is largely historical fiction, her reproduction of the text of Seattle's speech is attributed to Smith's actual translation. Since she interrupts the speech with fictionalized asides, the paragraphing of the speech printed here deviates somewhat from hers. Also, paragraphs 8 and 22 come from a version of the speech supplied by the University Library at the University of California Berkeley, which in most other respects, with the exception of paragraphing, resembles Anderson's version. Finally, where Anderson uses italics, I do not.

2 [Indian Superintendent of the Washington Territory, Isaac I. Stevens.]

black paint, it denotes that their hearts are black — and then they are often cruel and relentless, and our old men and old women are unable to restrain them. Thus it has ever been. Thus it was when the white man first began to push our forefathers westward. But let us hope that the hostilities between us may never return. We would have everything to lose and nothing to gain. Revenge by young braves is considered gain, even at the cost of their own lives, but old men who stay at home in times of war, and mothers who have sons to lose, know better.

Our Good Father at Washington — for I presume he is now our father, as well as yours, since Kling[3] George has moved his boundaries farther north — our Great and Good Father, I say, sends us word that if we do as he wishes he will protect us. His brave warriors will be to us a bristling wall of strength. His wonderful ships of war will fill our harbors. Then our ancient enemies far to the northward — the Haida and Tsimshian — will cease to frighten our women, children, and old men. Then in reality will he be our father — and we be his children.

But can that ever be?

No! Your god is not our god! Your god loves your people and hates mine. He folds his protecting arms about the pale-face and leads him by the hand as father leads infant son. But He has forgotten His red children — if they are really His.

Our god — the Great Spirit — seems to have forsaken us!

Your God makes your people wax strong every day. Soon they will fill all the land! Our people are ebbing away like a rapidly receding tide that will never return. The white man's God cannot love our people or he would protect them. They seem to be orphans who can look nowhere for help!

How can we be brothers? How can your God become our God and renew our prosperity? How can He awaken in us dreams of greatness?

If we have a common Heavenly Father, He must be partial — for He came to His paleface children. We Indians never saw Him. He gave you laws but had no words for us — His red children. Our teeming multitudes once filled this vast continent — as stars fill the firmament.

[3] [Anderson must use this spelling to suggest Chief Seattle's pronunciation of the word.]

No! We are two different races. We have separate origins and separate destinies. There is little in common between us!

To us the ashes of our ancestors are sacred. Their resting place is hallowed ground. You wander far from the graves of your ancestors and seemingly without regret.

Your religions are written on tables of stone by the iron finger of your God so you could not forget. The red man could never comprehend nor remember it. Our religion is the traditions of our ancestors — the dreams of our old men, given them in solemn hours of night by the Great Spirit. And the vision of our sachems is written in our hearts.

Your dead cease to love you and the land of their nativity as soon as they pass the portals of the tomb and wander beyond the stars. They are soon forgotten and never return. Our dead never forget the beautiful world that gave them being. They still love its verdant valleys, its murmuring rivers, its magnificent mountains, sequestered vales, and tree-rimmed lakes. They ever yearn, in tender affection, over the lonely-hearted living. Often they return from the Happy Hunting Ground to visit, guide, console, and comfort.

Day and night cannot dwell together. The red man has ever fled the approach of the white man, as morning mist flees the rising sun.

However, your proposition seems fair, and I think that my folks will accept it and will retire to the reservation you offer them. Then we will dwell apart in peace for the words of the Great White Chief seem to be the voice of Nature speaking to my people out of dense darkness.

It matters little where we pass the remnant of our days. They will not be many! The Indians' night promises to be dark. Not a single star of hope hovers above his horizon. Sad-voiced winds moan in the distance. Grim fate is on the red man's trail. Wherever he goes he will hear the approaching footsteps of his fell destroyer. He will prepare stolidly to meet his doom, as does the wounded doe at the footsteps of the approaching hunter.

A few more moons. A few more winters — and not one of the descendents of the mighty hosts that once moved over this broad land will be left. Once my people lived in happy homes and felt protected by the Great Spirit. Soon none will remain to mourn over the graves of a people once more powerful and hopeful than yours.

But why should I mourn the untimely fate of my people? Tribe follows tribe, and nation follows nation, like the waves of the sea. It is the order of nature, and regret is useless. Your time of decay may be distant, but — it will surely come. Even the white man whose God walked and talked with him — as friend to friend — cannot escape the common destiny. We may be brothers, after all. We shall see!

We will ponder your propositions. When we decide we will let you know.

But should we accept it, I here and now make this condition: that you permit us, at any time, to visit — without molestation — the tombs of our ancestors, friends, and children.

Every part of this soil is sacred in the estimation of my people. Every hillside, every valley, every plain and grove, has been hallowed by some happy or sad event in days long vanished. . . . Even rocks — which seem to be dumb and dead as they swelter in the sun along the silent shore — thrill with memories, and sympathize with my people. The very dust upon which you now stand responds more lovingly to their footsteps than to yours. It is rich with the blood of our ancestors, and our bare feet are more conscious of the sympathetic touch.

Our departed braves, fond mothers, glad, happy-hearted maidens, and even the little children who lived here and rejoiced here for a brief season, love these somber solitudes. At eventide they will become shadowy, returning spirits.

And when the last red man shall have perished — and the memory of my tribe is but a myth among white men — these shores will swarm with the invisible dead of my tribe. When your children's children think themselves alone in the field, the store, the shop, upon the highway, or in the silence of the pathless woods, they will not be alone. In all the earth there is no place dedicated to solitude.

At night — when the streets of your cities and villages are deserted — they will throng with the returning hosts that once filled them and still love this beautiful land.

The white man will never be alone!

Let the white man be just and deal kindly with my people,

for the dead are not powerless! Dead, did I say? There is no death — only a change of worlds!

This speech, even as it comes through Smith's stilted translation, is a potent text on the relatedness of all that lives and moves within the cycles of human life, and on the relationship of the red man to the white man in particular, even across the boundaries of life and death and time. In opposition to an American ideal of the rugged individual who is not respectful of the land and who remains alone and separate even from his ancestors, Seattle says, "In all the earth there is no place dedicated to solitude. . . . We may be brothers after all."

The consciousness of unity embedded in the speech evokes that moral sword that we, recreated in Seneca Falls, need to raise and thump on the big mahogany desks of all those who do not understand the spiritual technology of the web of life of black, red, white, and yellow, men and women, earth and sky, of which Seattle speaks.

Sam Keen notes that "being a man has always had something to do with being an outlaw, a thief, a heaven-stormer, an enemy of the established order" (105). A man who truly departs for Seneca Falls does become an outlaw. The established order of mass disregard for the natural environment, of uneasy complacency toward racial prejudice, and of long-standing tolerance of misogyny is superbly violated by the criminals of Seneca Falls, and by their ongoing descendents who would carry forward a Third Revolution.

The person who travels to Seneca Falls takes for herself or himself some of the very foundry fires of this heavily industrialized, pump-producing burg by which Elizabeth Cady Stanton and Frederick Douglass melted steel rods and recast them into the votive beams of a new earth household. We are free to take this fire into the far reaches of human community and into the complex and subtle web of the natural environment, prepared, all of us, to be called thieves and criminals for breaking the code of the predominant, traditional, but toxic, order. The new man and woman can use the light of Seneca Falls as a new kind of weapon to penetrate and transform every human institution, every unscrupulous developer's mind, every casual conversation, and every relationship, thereby changing every atom in the webs of the planet.

CHAPTER FOURTEEN

The Ghost in the Machine

I grew up just as the Industrial Revolution was imperceptibly giving way. Where were the rituals that might have oriented me in a mythic way toward women and blacks, toward the natural environment, or toward some conception of the totality of the planet? All I learned was that I was a citizen of the greatest country on earth. All I had to do was get educated, preferably in engineering or science, and the world would be mine. Whatever the spiritual or social issues current between men and women, whatever the concerns of the theologians or psychologists or feminists of the time, they simply did not filter down to my 1950s classrooms or our dinner table on Johnston Street. Progress was infinite, and if I brushed my teeth with flouride and did well in school, I, too, would be swept along to success.

More than most small towns of the region, the Seneca Falls of the mid-1800s was jammed with industry, and a large work force of no-nonsense men guided its textile shuttles, ground the flour of its many mills, and poured the molten metal of its fire engine and pump works — men with little or no education who greased the wheels, worked long shifts, and provided pork and flour for their families.

When I was growing up after the Second World War, Seneca Falls had five booming factories: Goulds Pumps, Sylvania, Seneca Falls Machine, Seneca Knitting Mills, and Westcott Rule. And it still has a theme of brute, blue-collar strength; a large segment of the Seneca Falls population is comprised of industrial workers, men and women who live by the time clock, who are governed by tight rules of seniority and shifts, union dues and overtime. The town remains chock full of plants and shops that require rugged workers to operate, boasts of passionate soccer and football fans, and lives with an almost-abandoned downtown, lots of pizza places, one-hundred-year-old buildings that hardly anyone appreciates, a nearly stagnant canal, and almost no memory of Elizabeth Cady Stanton.

I was slowly seduced in my home town during the fifties by the searing age of technology. Like the children of other industrial towns of the Northeast, I was falsely initiated into what feminists would later call "patriarchal technology" — the tribal laws of belief in infinite technological advancement and the eternal supremacy of the shiny American Dream. Only in retrospect can I discern the mechanical hand of outmoded technological values as it tirelessly reached out to process me.

As a kid I observed the robot stares of factory workers walking and driving to and from the Sylvania plant located at the end of my street. The boys and girls from the other side of town, the offspring of factory workers, seemed somehow hardened, as if they themselves had become like machines. Cars, satellites, and televisions were the symbols of my coming of age. These images of technology were indelibly tattooed on my young soul as the ritual by which I would be initiated into manhood.

I remember pausing outside the old Strand Theatre from time to time to read the New York State historical sign commemorating the place of the First Woman's Rights Convention. The seven-foot sign was embedded in cement along the sidewalk of Fall Street, across from the billiard hall and the railroad car diner. The site of the Wesleyan Chapel was a laundromat. And I can remember, on my way to and from the movies on Saturday afternoons or weekend evenings, seeing frazzled-looking women with their children going in and out of that laundromat, looking different from my mother.

These harried women who looked so toughened yet weakened as well were factory workers; some were the offspring of farmers who had left their farms to find better-paying jobs

in our industrialized village. The kids were usually unwind-
ing on the side street along the laundromat, running in
between parked trucks, setting up scenes of contest and war,
and, uneasily for me, somehow different from my friends and
my brothers. The billiard hall and the all-night diner were the
gathering places of shift workers and bullies, and this gritty
crossroads was where the quiet waters of Seneca Falls's resi-
dential neighborhoods met the uncertain turbulence of a
sleazy news shop and a taxi stand. The diner was at the top
of the hill that led down into the lower depths along the
Seneca River Canal, where the knitting mills shuttled twenty-
four hours a day. The kids along the side street by the laundromat seemed already grown-up, completed, their destinies
written on their brass foreheads and across the backs of their
dirty hands.

When I walked from my part of town, cool and free, past
these straits of a different time and place, I didn't know
enough to realize that I was coming not only from another
side of town but from a different class, a different economic
order, a different destiny. We lived first on Johnston Street
and then on nearby Cayuga Street, where huge elms joined
their fingers overhead to shelter my family from the filth of
the factory, the hard regimen of shift work and labor/man-
agement politics, and the cynicism of spirit that so many
assembly lines seem to engender. Television more than my
parents schooled me about class and taught me the totems
of material wealth. Television taught us kids the images of
immaculate modern kitchens, the sociological importance of
the right cars, and the urgency of acquiring the latest gad-
gets and toys.

During these years there were cars that I disdainfully
called model A's, the black boxes on slim tires that still
whirred back and forth from the Sylvania plant. Since they
failed to meet the standard of the new cars advertised on television, when my friends and I would see one we'd yell,
"Jalopy!" and contemptuously throw gravel at it. And we
watched, my friends and I, along Johnston Street as the first

Sylvania shift let out at three o'clock in the afternoon, and the cars lined up for a third of a mile, from the plant to the corner at Cayuga Street. The Sylvania workers, some on foot, looked weary, bullied, and bullying. They carried lunch boxes. They wore blue working-man's shirts and heavy black shoes, and their faces were frozen in industrial resignation.

Next door to us lived three elderly sisters, the Woodworths, in a very weathered, nineteenth-century home, with an outhouse in the back, set next to a pile of egg shells and ashes from the huge Franklin stove that heated their parlor. The outhouse sent up pathetic flags of odor, especially in the summertime, on into the 1960s, and the kids in the neighborhood muttered epithets because the Woodworths did not have a modern bathroom. The older boys of the neighborhood, including my brother, festooned their porch with toilet paper and trash for not being contemporary enough.

Most of my childhood memories are anchored on natural things invaded and humiliated by technological menace. I lived up the street from the DelRussos, whose father had a hook instead of a right hand, and near the Coffees, whose father had been crippled by falling into a grease pit at an automotive garage. There was the wounded crow that had been shot by my brother with a BB gun, the crippled squirrel nursed in a box, our dog that was chloroformed in our garage while my brother cried. There was a snapping turtle put on display by neighborhood ruffians, the cow bones down a bank at the edge of a field, and the Chinese pheasants that strutted golden and indigo in a too-small cage on the property next to my grandmother's backyard. I can remember the eagerly awaited arrival on summer evenings of the mosquito-spraying jeep. Mr. Simpson, the county engineer, would drive into my neighborhood spraying great clouds of anti-mosquito liquid, and my brothers and I and our friends would run behind the jeep and glory in the magic cloud of the spray that might very well have been DDT.

Our bicycles were balloon-tired, American-made, and we humped them around on the broken cement sidewalks, over curbs, and up and down roadside paths that kids and bikes grind into the ground. I graduated from the old-fashioned, hand-powered, reel-type lawn mower to a massive, cheap gas-powered rotary. I dragged my father out of the house to assist me with getting the thing started, and from then on I cut nearly anything that would fit under its huge, shiny tin lip. My BB gun became an extension of my sand shovel. It was literally a way of reaching out and manipulating my environment, from a distance. Unfortunately, I shot a robin, a phoebe, and countless starlings, carelessly, intuitively, from the hip. I shot at yellowjackets, moths, and even nodules of amber oozing from a cherry tree, and I can remember the sound of my BBs bouncing off the sides of squirrels.

Cayuga Street, which ran into the village of Seneca Falls, was closer to the twentieth century than Johnston Street. It was in a different country where cars went fast, refusing to stop for balls that rolled into the street, where drivers and passengers might send expletives hurtling at me and my friends like butcher knives as we rode our bikes innocently along the walk.

I felt out of place in the industrial tumbler of Seneca Falls. I was unconsciously looking for passionate souls, the poets among the pump makers, the young and the restless among the yarn spinners of the local textile industry. I tried going to the billiard hall. I went to drive-ins, to the roller rink, to the local state park to hang out in the pavilion. I went to high school football games, to little league, to the aborted Saturday morning soccer league. I tried hunting and ice skating. I worked summers in the mills and factories from the summer of my sophomore year of high school. I swept out bins of yarn, cut old wool into salvageable pieces, lifted and boxed thousands of Sylvania television picture tubes. I listened to the workers describe their wives, listened to off-color jokes, smoked on my breaks, punched my time card, and smelled the factory air.

I am positive I was searching unconsciously for my soul, the ghost in the machine, the spiritual spring inside the time clock that wrapped its constricting hands around the forehead of almost everyone who lived in Seneca Falls. Like all young men who grow up and do the things that kids do — work in the summer, play sports, discover girls — I was looking for some reference point on an inner map that might tell me who I was, where I was going and by what route. But I kept bumping into the granite foundations of the factories of Seneca Falls.

Unlike Elizabeth Cady Stanton, I did not achieve in Seneca Falls a vision of the way things were supposed to be. I understood physical strength, and youth, and the thumping of sexuality. I understood kisses, and popularity, and winning football games. I understood the glorious object of sexual intercourse. I understood looking good and having a million friends. I understood cool and reticence, and understatement, and gesture. I understood how the man says the minimum and the woman fills in the emotional details. I understood that it was necessary to work hard without a word of complaint. But nothing informed me that I had to grab hold of the infinite in some way to make life complete. I needed a sense of meaning more ultimate than what I could suck from the lips of young women, from pizza, or from the pervasive technological hum of the American machine. So while I was being subtly but falsely initiated into the marvelous modern state of science and technology by the tribal leaders of advertising, I was receiving no instruction in the character sources of spirit. My relatives didn't provide it, the friends of my parents didn't offer it, and my teachers and coaches didn't seem to know about it either. Television didn't even try.

In the classroom I was taught logarithms, the workings of Congress, and how to say thank you in a European tongue. Outside the classroom, my friends and I inhaled the smoke of sex and spoke the codes of covert fun, all of which rushed in to fill the vacuums of our unbuilt but haunted, spiritual spaces. But strangely, as cheap thrills usually over-powered the gentler excitements of scholarship, they never completely drowned out the murmur of the soul. My inner-most heart was forever being towed into hyperspace by the smell of crushed violets in my brain, which seemed to origi-nate in another country altogether. I felt a kind of fire in my chest cavity and lacked the language to express its heat. This fire seemed to be fed by my sexual musings and by my occa-sional intellectual accomplishments in school, but the fire I felt was mostly a yearning to understand how the universe was put together, and where I was on its map. While I sensed the compass of my heart point down and in toward this fire, the real meaning of my life seemed always just out of reach, like a flower sealed in glass. I had no teacher in flowers or fires.

I went to college, where I drifted far out, with much wine, lots of cigarettes, girlfriends, all-night parties chaperoned by the lyrics of Bob Dylan, drunken dancing, poetry scribbled on scrap paper, keg parties on the roof of the fraternity house, and still the feeling of missing something grew more and more fierce, fanned by alcohol and the passing skirts of coeds. I questioned every dogma, stopped taking my father's advice, sneaked around, lied, went cold toward members of my family, slept all day, smoked three packs of cigarettes daily, craved alcohol, bought a motorcycle against my father's counsel and wasn't smart enough to repair it when it caught fire, lost the pristine vigor of my robust health, and demanded answers from an unjust world. I looked for the meaning of it all. I grappled for it everywhere, in the curves of women's bodies, in the villages of their genitals. I looked for it in the heavy smoke of Lucky Strikes, in the cool lyrics of Joni Mitchell, in countless bottles of Gallo. I looked for north, east, south, and west in women's hair, in their easy, sun-on-water laughter, in their narrow, weak hands, in the subtle swaying of their breasts as they walked to history class in the spring.

I looked everywhere for the map of what it all meant, for a legend by which I could measure the distances and put it all into perspective. I found bits and pieces, but largely they were illusions, as they were always found floating in beer and wine, and in a tobacco haze. Wine was my spiritual source and sexuality my communion. This was the life I led for five or six years after I graduated from high school, perhaps having been the most popular kid in the world, having been president of my class for three years out of four, on my way to certain success.

I squandered my powers. My family was not religious, and we didn't have the aphorisms of uncles and aunts. We didn't have significant family traditions, rituals or gatherings or dinner parties where adults would say what they knew, if not for the benefit of each other than for the benefit of the young. There was no wrestling with God, no heart-to-heart talks in which hurt and tragedy and weakness were revealed, bound up, and healed brother to brother, uncle to nephew, cousin to cousin. There was no common understanding in my family about what was beautiful, what was real, what was worth sacrificing for to the nth degree.

Certainly we had intelligence, no lack of articulate conversation, and an awareness of the news and world events. There was a large theatre manager's hook applied to cheap ambition and flashy personalities, and all cheaters, liars, and bullies were generally condemned. There was an intellectual and ethical sense of right and wrong that would probably have qualified me for any boy scout troop in the world. In fact, my father is a particularly honest, moral man who is generous, patient, and kind. And some of these more noble virtues did rub off on me and became rudimentary navigational tools, but they were finally overwhelmed by the lack of a deep-sea chart, the absence of a blueprint of how a man, I, should proceed. For the intelligence and virtue of my family were based on nothing more than rational, deductive logic, and a certain detachment that comes naturally to historians and smart, fallen Protestants.

I am grateful for what my family gave me, for it did provide me with a sanctuary for the purpose of observation and intellectual judgment. In the granite of Seneca Falls, it carved out a place of relative safety. But I needed a larger and clearer map, with some reference to the giddy stars, the unworldly sound of waterfalls, to love, to the Great Spirit, and the golden cord that attaches to spiritual truth. I needed a way to put the head, the heart, and the hand together into some kind of symmetry, and I didn't know where to begin. If there was something called spirituality, I had no idea of what it was or where it was marked on the map of becoming a man. And as a man from Seneca Falls, I would become fascinated with what it means to be a male from this hard-edged, masculine, but forever women's place.

Mind in its precision and clarity would not be invented in me until I entered graduate school. Up until then, I had swum in the shapeless sea of emotion and would-be soul, and not at all with the help of the sextant of the mind. That's the way I preferred it, I guess. In graduate school, I studied English and taught English composition to college freshmen. Robert Frost's essay "Education by Poetry: A Meditative Monologue" became a personal favorite.

Frost speaks of two distinct forces in the human psyche. The first is enthusiasm, the kind that bubbles up naturally and powerfully in response to a sunset or a powerful poem, which he calls "sunset raving." He considers this enthusiasm the starting point, the raw energy of the life force, feminine in the sense that it is based in feeling. To be of any worth, he tells us, this enthusiasm has to be passed through the constraints of an idea, through the "prism of the intellect and spread on a screen in a color" (192). He called this "prism of the intellect" a metaphor. For Frost, this is the process of thinking; to think is to have ways of comparing one thing with the other, to have the prism and lens of metaphor by which to tame, educate, and disperse the raw energy of enthusiasm and emotion. Education by poetry, he called it, since poetry is the warehouse of civilization's metaphors.

Two distinct aspects combine here, like a lion leaping through a burning steel hoop. The rudderless but powerful surges of the emotions, which are the stuff of the feminine soul and of adolescence and young adulthood, are understood to leap through the steel, or the machine-like aspect of the mind, thereby fulfilling and humanizing the mind.

I liked this way of defining thinking. I understood it to mean that my self-development had everything to do with deciding on the most appropriate metaphors, and then letting them act as intellectual conduits for my emotions. If I could pass the blind and mad enthusiasms of my flailing emotions through the cold prism of my mind, my life would be free to express color and brilliance. Like the scarecrow in the Emerald City, I had, with the help of the wizard Frost, acquired a mind. More importantly, I would come to discover that when the raw enthusiasm of emotion does get tamed, filtered, and prismed by the intellect, a personal transformation is possible, a third dimension is manifested, spirit inheres.

Frost's suggestion of passing one's enthusiasm through a metaphor supplied the rudimentary map I needed for achieving my own personal balance. In this one brief essay, I had found a way of melding what were two distinct aspects of being human. Most of us, men and women, are either heavy in intellect or overly endowed with enthusiasm. They had become two separate aspects in my life, and I suspect that most people in Western civilization are similarly halved. I had always had a raw, ungovernable enthusiasm for life. I was, in Frost's terms, a "sunset raver."

For me, Seneca Falls was a community where the mind was vigorously at work building products and machines in the best tradition of the scientific method and the Industrial Revolution. So I had ducked out of Seneca Falls, without being fully initiated into its stark, industrial values, the hard, distancing rationality of our scientific and secular age. I was very much a spiritual sensualist, a blind poet of the emotions, an arrogant and comical dreamer, looking for love in among car graveyards, so to speak. I was squirming as a nonbeliever under the era's oppressive scientific ambience. Here is a poem I wrote in Seneca Falls that tries to explain.

ONCE A SPIRIT MEADOW, AMERICA

In Simone's car graveyard, I drive my holy mind, try to find the way out

Hub cap is snagged like a snuffer above flames of black-eyed susans, clutch-plate nestled beside wild flox

I place a greasy transmission box steeple-like over an Indian paint brush, flower breathes freely within gears

I sense an impending miracle in the steel mills of America, slag heaps blasted by tulips

I shine a chrome bumper with my breath, see a vision of a holy man and a mechanical engineer locking arms, jigging on the edge of a cliff

My heart eddies like the sea within the steel hulls of studebakers

I don't talk about the price of steel or the standard of living, I'm taciturn as the mud in the fist of lilacs

Above I hear thousands of migrating geese; I would like to build a factory around them, cast the enthusiasm of their voices into the molds of American English

Down on my hands and knees, I arrange thrown-off car parts into the semblance of a rose

Enclosed within the psychic walls of industry, I remember edifices have shifted from the growth of trees

I talk to God through the steel horns of manifolds

At the hub of the vicious circle of bloodied windshields, crumpled paper of steel fenders, I call out, confess my brotherhood to the engines of snowflakes

America has poured its iron into weapons and cars; I tip the ladle of rain clouds into the wooden bowl of my heart

I'm out here wandering through steel carcasses, starving for something for which I don't have a name

I uncover a rusty radio beneath crab grass, hear the children of the world singing

A car door severed like a wing on the earth; I open it, crawl into the driver's seat of flowers

In school we are taught to think like industry: speed, efficiency, profit; we have to learn on our own to be beautiful as uncut grass

I drive blind through the cyclone fences in which factories are wrapped

I never successfully passed my mad enthusiasm through the particular hoop of machine-dominated Seneca Falls. I ran away from home with only emotional intensity tied up in my bundle, with a warm and vulnerable heart but no protective mind at all. And I remained uninitiated into the scientific age for years. This happened in part because my father never made any attempt at so initiating me. He was inherently suspicious of machines. He never owned a typewriter, never worked on his car, never bought a screwdriver, never repaired the family's bicycles, was baffled by the fuse box, and never fixed a damn thing. When I had asked him to go to the garage to help me start the new lawn mower, he was helpless.

So I was uninvited into the twentieth century. I was prodded by psychometric batteries and measured by thousands of multiple-choice tests. I was coached by subliminal advertising. I was thus ritually invited by my elders and teachers into the community of science and the secular age. But I refused that image of what it was to become a man. I was a warm, sexual, spiritual being floating like a milkweed, closer and closer to the engines and gears and furnaces of the factory, and I was doomed. As an undergraduate in college, I crashed and burned like a naive, blind, sensual monk.

With Frost's lesson, I was born again. It now seemed clear that it was not the mind itself that was responsible for tyranny and war, class hatred and racism, and the annihilation of all that was mysterious and dark. No, the evils of civilization as produced by its best minds were a result of the intellect operating in a vacuum, without being informed by human feeling, without being tempered by the enthusiasm of "sunset ravers" like me, without its masculine products being feminized by more spiritual, human aspects.

I began to understand that it was my responsibility as a man to discover those metaphors that would permit me to develop a mind that was incisive and logical and penetrating, but one that was also driven by poetry and fire, and love. Beginning with the dozens of texts it was my responsibility to read and understand as a graduate student and a graduate teaching assistant in English, I began to acquire such a mind. And with marriage and the steady influence my wife provided, her sturdy advice, her powerful, open heart toward me, I began to coordinate myself enough to begin spinning on my own axis. I began to center, to go inward in the safety of my wife's routines of love. Having read Frost's essay, I acquired a mind of my own. Other influential readings at the time, which deepened my appreciation for forging mind with feeling, were Ken Kesey's *One Flew Over the Cuckoo's Nest,* Thoreau's *Walden,* and Robert Pirsig's *Zen and the Art of Motorcycle Maintenance.*

These literary treatments represented vividly my struggle to integrate my ungovernable and more feminine emotions with the angular, sharp, mechanical aspect of the masculine mind of the twentieth century. I made this all my own personal business. I was convinced the task of integrating my two functions of mind and heart, masculine and feminine, represented the most difficult human task ever, a process that was imperative for American men.

But as hard as I tried, the Niagara Falls flow of my emotions would overwhelm. My mind would play catch-up, reacting in the peculiar ways typical of a threatened despot, inappropriately controlling or inappropriately distant, spacey, and remote. Not until I reached my forties did I begin to achieve a kind of balance and unity between these elements. I acquired the ability to be present in the here and now, not needing to cover up by exaggerating one function over another, or hiding one from the other. In my forties, I like to think I have become capable of thinking intelligently while still possessing a wasteful and generous heart.

If it had not been for a recovered function of mind, I would have withered and died as a holdover hippie without a clue, with only a sympathetic and pacifist heart to my name, flattened by the ordinary commerce of men and women. The capacity of my mind to will and apply itself under adverse conditions is married now to an undercurrent of soul. I visualize my reckless, emotional, and feminine energy as rising vertically from the earth itself, up into my toes and legs and with shapely discipline blooming up through the treelike stem of my spine into the branches of the twirling knives of my rational brain. I am protected at my soul sources and connected, after a fashion, with the world at large. I feel like a power source, and just like Kesey's Randall P. McMurphy, the power rams up through and makes all of me dance at center. I became a Green Man, a prince of spring. I have become spiritual.

Tutored by Elizabeth Cady Stanton and Frederick Douglass, my feminine aspect has become more courageous, my masculine more moral. I flash a sword of consciousness toward all that is fractured, ready to cut up and bind up. I am Elizabeth Cady Stanton with antlers, Frederick Douglass holding up a perfect hoop of fire inviting the cold citizenry to jump through against their wishes, to hold hands around a mystic center.

CHAPTER FIFTEEN

Seneca Falls as Metaphor:
Spiritual Waters and Goulds Pumps

We have seen that the hamlet of Seneca Falls, the center of the Six Nations of the Iroquois, is situated along what had become known as the "psychic highway" of the reform age. In addition to its world-embracing pump industry, Seneca Falls saw the pumping from deep within the New World of a tremendous spiritual, indigenous, reformist impulse. Historians have called the area of western New York to which Seneca Falls is central, the "Burned-Over District." During the first half of the nineteenth century it was caught in a conflagration of reform activity: the movements for revival, temperance, abolition, and woman's rights swept through the area like wildfire. Charles Grandison Finney, a famed traveling preacher of the time, had a strong influence on the character of Henry Stanton, who would become the husband of Elizabeth Cady. William Lloyd Garrison made his way through the region frequently, and Frederick Douglass edited the *North Star* in nearby Rochester.

The historian Whitney R. Cross describes this frenetic part of the world:

> Across the rolling hills of western New York and along the line of DeWitt Clinton's famed canal, there stretched in the second quarter of the nineteenth century a "psychic highway." Upon this broad belt of land congregated a people extraordinarily given to unusual religious beliefs, peculiarly devoted to crusades aimed at the perfection of mankind and the attainment of millennial happiness. Few of the enthusiasms or eccentricities of this generation of Americans failed to find exponents here.

Most of them gained rather greater support here than else-where. Several originated in the region. (3)

Cross characterizes the emigrant Yankees of this region as filled with a "moral intensity" that evokes the hippie gen-eration of the 1960s, young, restless, and eager to break free of the stultifying embrace of the relatively staid lifestyles of their families back in New England:

> This wholesale emigration served to select a group of trans-planted Yankees who would be on the whole more sensitive to religious influences than their kinfolk in the homeland. Those who went west were, first of all, younger sons for whom the scrubby farms held little opportunity. The youths, too, had greater ambition and lust for adventure than their elders, who either had substantial stakes and compelling social ties in the old land or had already compromised upon mere existence in the hard struggle for a competence. Although two-thirds of all Vermonters were twenty-five or under in 1800, the emigrants were, on the average, still younger. (6)

By the mid-1800s, Cross notes, "the benevolent groups had succeeded . . . in creating a phenomenally intensive reli-gious and moral awareness in the Burned-Over District" (28–29).

The 1825 completion of the Erie Canal and the subse-quent great increase in economic activity throughout central New York contributed to scattered "episodic eccentricities" as well as to "significant enthusiasms" (55). Cross points to two Shaker communities along the psychic highway of the Burned-Over area, as well as to the colony of the Universal Friend on Keuka Lake and the Mormons. In almost every way, the imagination of the populace seemed poised for moral and intellectual adventure. Legends of treasure buried in the area by Captain Kidd flourished at the time.

There were castigations of "cold" clergymen, and much time and energy was devoted to engineering revivals. New dietary laws sprang up under the rubric of Grahamism. The care of "wayward women" and prostitutes attracted much heated public discussion. In describing Charles Grandison Finney, Cross says,

> His eminence lay not so much in what he did as in the striking way he had of doing it. The wedding of humanitarian movements and revivalism followed upon a lengthy betrothal. . . . The rampant optimism of the period was the cupid who whispered that this ceremony would consummate happiness for all in the approaching millennium. Such a union could blot out every remaining sin which stood between man and perfection. . . . Charles Grandison Finney, probably aware of . . . the preferment to be gained . . . if the ceremony went smoothly, was the minister. (168)

In the 1820s, Theodore Weld, later a friend of Elizabeth Cady Stanton, tried to raise funds for the Oneida Institute and its "system of education that would introduce the Millennium" (168). Douglass began publishing the *North Star* in the 1840s, and the *Rochester Observer* had been expressing strong antislavery sentiment since the early 1830s.

The antislavery movement blended with the religious enthusiasms of the place. As Cross describes it:

> The Burned-Over District seized leadership in the abolition crusade, and the consequent influence of this region upon the enlarged agitation of the forties and fifties and upon the Civil War itself, constitutes the most important single contribution of western New York's enthusiastic mood to the main currents of national history. (217)

The Millerites, who believed in the literal return of Christ in 1844, were active in the area: "Probably well over fifty thousand people in the United States became convinced that time would run out in 1844, while a million or more of their fellows were skeptically expectant" (287). Even when the date came and went, the group's leader, William Miller, was able to maintain his faith. In a letter in 1845, he said he would be satisfied with "anything which will prove Christ near, and the nearer the better" (312).

Other "enthusiasms and eccentricities" were an active phrenologist movement, hundreds of American Swedenborgians, followers of mesmerism, land reformers, and men and women who practiced various forms of communal living, including free love. The Fourier Movement gained momentum in the forties, and its advocates lectured in Seneca Falls, preaching a kind of universal religion that had as its mission sobriety and social justice. It succeeded in establishing communes mostly in the immediate Rochester area. The local Hicksite Quakers contributed important members and support to the struggle for women's rights. All lived and worked in the context of a millennialist consciousness in the Seneca Falls region.

The village's earliest commercial activity was marked in the late 1700s, when its earliest settler, Job Smith, helped westward-traveling pioneers and their families cross the river, or maneuver up and around the falls and rapids. It is said that Smith himself was not a particularly upright citizen, and that he might even have been a fugitive from justice, hiding among the Indians.

In 1862, Henry Stowell, a Seneca Falls newspaperman and compiler of a local chronology, describes Smith:

> He came up the Mohawk and Seneca Rivers, subsisting on corn pounded in a mortar, together with wild game and salmon from the river, which were then very abundant. A traveler who, with his party, passed up the river in 1788–9, and were assisted by him over the Falls, represented him as living alone, owning a yoke of oxen, carrying on a small traffic with the Indians — and, in transporting the boats of the party around the Falls, used a cart, the wheels of which were sawed entire from logs. (2)

Soon dams and mills were built to harness the water power, and any number of mills began to operate. According to Stowell:

Our village may not boast of its authors, poets and statesmen, or its Colleges and halls of learning, yet few places surpass it in its manufacturing interests, in the enterprise and public spirit of its inhabitants, and in the energy, tact and indomitable perseverance of its business men. Here manufacturing and the mechanic arts flourish and prosper. (2)

By the 1790s, Seneca Falls had become a borough of about 300 inhabitants, and included several mills and blacksmith and cooper shops. Lawrence Van Cleef, the second settler after Job Smith, was an early entrepreneur, as was Colonel Wilhelmus Mynderse. Soon there would be a saw mill, a plaster-of-paris quarry, a harness shop, and a tannery. The textile industry began in 1806 with a fulling mill for cloth dressing and carding. A set of locks and a canal system was completed in 1816. Undeveloped land was freed up along the river in 1825; inns were built and an industrial boom began.

A paper mill followed, and in 1830 a machine shop and furnace were established on the banks of the river, producing plows and threshing machines. In 1848 an iron works sprang up in the flood plain of the Seneca River known as "the flats," near the heart of the village of Seneca Falls, and began manufacturing axes and edge tools. The manufacture of pumps began in 1839 and "has been the great element of our prosperity" (22). Various manufacturing partnerships joined in the making of all manner of pumps, both wooden and iron; the first iron pump was cast in Seneca Falls in 1844. The technology developed in making pumps became central to the manufacture of fire engines, also a Seneca Falls industry. A local historical publication of 1904 put the number of current employees at the Seneca Woolen Mills, established in 1844, at 175, with three shifts operating and five thousand dollars in monthly wages expended.

Goulds Pumps, the leading manufacturer and world exporter of the water-immersible pump, began operation in 1848. The process of melting metal has not changed much in these one hundred and fifty years; the Goulds foundry today is still a hell-like world of fire and smoke where husky men working on dirt floors pour vats of molten metal, glowing orange and red, into expertly shaped sand molds. Above, a massive industrial crane rolls back and forth on railroad-size tracks, through the noxious fumes gathered in the high cathedral ceilings. When the molten steel is poured, clouds of steam hiss up like the exhalations of dragons. The men at their respective work stations look like Neanderthals huddled in a dreamscape of fire and smoke. The squeal of the crane, the shouts and curses of the men, and the sounds of steel racking up against steel make a hard-edged music that permeates the foundry.

I worked in the foundry in 1979, and I can remember the "ox-man" who, it was said, had sex with his daughter and then held off the state police with a rifle. I can remember the harsh vocabulary used to refer to women as the mere receivers of men's sexuality. The code of conduct among us steelworkers was to act as much like steel as we possibly could, to be strong and inarticulate, except when flinging, like red-hot steel scraps, our barbs toward women and the rest of the world. No women worked at the foundry, and only one black man ever came through, on his way somewhere else. White men tipped the ton-heavy vats of molten steel into their womblike molds, stirred the car-sized tubs with long pokers, and skimmed the creamy scum from the tops of the boiling stuff.

One woman who worked elsewhere in the plant told me that occasionally she had to walk through the foundry to deliver packages to the other side. She said that when she had to do this she would have to prepare herself mentally to make the trek across this hellish place, and that as she walked, she prayed. She could feel the stares and the hungry souls lapping out toward her, as if Dante himself had sent her reluctantly on a mission to one of the devil's lowest levels (Miller, "World of Foundry," 22).

Here is a poem I wrote at the time of my foundry work:

FOUNDRY PRAYER

I pour molten metal, lift steel jackets and weights off poured molds, shake them out

I'd rather pour my heart-ladle into different words for love

I found a dead katydid in hopper of brass chips, ate venison shoulder cooked beside boiling iron

Cement floor of foundry is built on dark, sexual crib of roots

Who knows when green ganglia of trees will snap steel cables?

Besides brass and iron, I pour high loneliness into saucers of Queen Anne's lace growing unnoticed beneath rusty flasks

Shepherd Crane, big as a bridge, runs on rails hundred feet high, cuts laterally with sound of subway through sunbeams thick as men

Bearded, channelled face of foundry man illuminated with unmanufactured light falling through high cathedral windows

Within brick walls I whistle a tune that swirls up amongst pigeons strutting in minuets on high, unreachable windows

With long steel stick I pick red hot castings off conveyor, sling them into rusty bins

Foundry vault is buttressed by steel girders that flare out like tree branches

I follow Shepherd Crane, hook its chain up to copes and drags big as cars, send them up screeching

Under my arms, slabs of cold iron big as books, into the fire

Rhythm of machines, military, iron heels marching

Maybe there is a mold of tulip, wing, storm into which I can pour myself

I am a steel worker, my mind an empty meadow across which I keep running breathlessly to the sea

I'd rather be watching the ladle of the sea pour into the crevices of tide pools

I read strange, luminous script written in loops and verticals of
dandelion-shaped sparks, in the gassy vacuums the word
courage

Through high, grimey windows the color of miner's lungs, see
my way into quiet blue sky

And so it is Seneca Falls, as a showcase of the mind, of the
rational spirit of science and industry, along with the com-
plementarity of the ghostly manifestation of the feminine and
revolutionary spirit it exemplifies, that has come to represent the ultimate metaphor for my life as a man.

Looking back at my brief experience at the foundry, I see
it as a crucible for my life since then. I see Seneca Falls as
being at the eye of the technology needle through which
white men must pass, literally arm in arm with women and
blacks. There is no other door, no other exit into the twenty-
first century, except along the pyschic highway that leads
both in and out of Seneca Falls. If we white men are once and
for all to think and feel simultaneously, we must embrace and
integrate the sexual and racial unity we have been exploring
here, precisely within the modern industrial state. If we are to
be humanized and progress from this point on, it is the undifferentiated, feminine, electric soul-sea that flows underneath
us that now needs to gush up through the terrifying machinery of our minds.

The mind of the man who has been, in an intellectual and
spiritual sense, to Seneca Falls, is like one of those splendid
Goulds pumps. We, too, must draw on some underground
source to integrate the male/female, the black/white, and to
spit out the humanity so forged in a sun-shocked stream all
over the world.

CHAPTER SIXTEEN

Arrival:
The Vertical Dimension

Job Smith, reputed fugitive, lived clandestinely among the dwindling Indians along the Seneca River in the late 1700s and hauled the essential things of pioneering people across dangerous whitewater in a wobbly ox-cart. Those of us who want to reach Seneca Falls today — and arrive at our full humanity — must also cross a river, one that separates body from spirit, emotion from reason, black from white, woman from man. The wobbly ox-cart becomes the wobbly vessel of the self, a house of worship shaken from without and from within by the deep, dangerous waters of the feminine. To make such a perilous crossing takes faith. To arrive at Seneca Falls, at our center, means to come to terms with God.

At this point, for me, the criminal Job Smith gives way to the theologian Paul Tillich who gave me the blueprint of centering by which I could build, in the workshop of the soul, a spiritual ark for the crossing. Tillich taught me that the act of centering is the threefold marriage of reason, feeling, and will. He calls their conjunction faith: a "tension between the cognitive function of man's personal life, on the one hand, and emotion and will, on the other." Faith, he writes, "is the unity of every element in the centered self" (*Dynamics,* 8).

Tillich finds the precise description for the experience of a center. He calls it ecstasy — "standing outside of oneself" without ceasing to be oneself, with all elements united in the personal center. But, in addition to being ecstatic, free, and unified, the experience of faith is also dynamic and directed. Faith is a soul engine, with vertical and horizontal axes whirling and humming in the experience of Seneca Falls.

If I have done my work so far in looking into the faces of
Elizabeth Cady Stanton and Frederick Douglass, and if I have
duly crossed the river that forms the magic, paradoxical bar-
rier and found my vertical and horizontal bearings in the holy
spot of breakthrough, then I should be prepared to surrender to the shaking experience of center, in which soul naturally inheres. And, if Tillich is right, I should find at that center the living meaning of a faith connection to God, and
perhaps, something about the nature of American spirituality
as well.

An American male who becomes a man under the guiding hands of Elizabeth Cady Stanton and Frederick Douglass
takes his position on the horizontal continuum of social
awareness and community in a transformed relation to
women and blacks. He becomes a lover and a knower. Feminist psychologist Carol Gilligan writes of what such a radical repositioning demands: "[T]he underlying epistemology
. . . shifts from the Greek ideal of knowledge as a correspondence between mind and form to the Biblical conception of
knowing as a process of human relationship" (*In a Different
Voice*, 173).

But one's manhood is incomplete if it is achieved only in
relation to the community — especially the contemporary
American community, which has almost entirely forgotten
the vertical dimension that locates the center. Tillich says,
"Human existence is never without that which breaks vertically into it" (*New Being*, 121). The vertical dimension
points up toward mystery and down into a darkness of a
more personal kind, the undisciplined hell of one's own
unknowingness. Tillich specifically relates God to depth, to
what lies beneath the surface. "Truth is deep and not shallow; suffering is depth and not height" (*Shaking the Foundations*, 53). If the road to Seneca Fall is, finally, the road to
the vertical ascent of the spirit, it is rooted in our depth and
in the body, and we are bound to suffer along the way.

The map of Seneca Falls as center describes the magical
boundaries of the vertical and the horizontal, the

north/south, east/west of the soul, of home. But arriving at the center is one thing, undergoing the initiatory rites of passage that teach the soul how to inhabit its holy precincts is quite another.

Toward that end, I assert that Stanton's Declaration of Rights and Sentiments, together with the Resolutions passed at the convention (Appendices 1 and 2), are equivalent in spiritual magnitude to Martin Luther's posting of his ninety-five theses on the Castle church door in Wittenburg in 1517, a deed that initiated Western European humanity into a new consciousness. Just as Luther's epoch-making questioning of the Pope's right to absolve sins on the basis of money payments known as indulgences challenged papal authority, so Stanton and her cohorts challenged the hegemony of male authority rooted in Christian tradition. Not surprisingly, both of these challenges to the existing theological center took place in a church. In both cases, the fight was on.

Erik Erikson studied Luther psychoanalytically in *Young Man Luther,* using the example of this erstwhile Catholic monk to demonstrate the fullest resolution of his theory of identity crisis. Luther's identity crisis was resolved by history itself, in the Reformation, which he instigated. And the Reformation, by planting the seeds of individual freedom and individual access to God through conscience, provoked an identity crisis for European civilization as a whole that led eventually to the rise of the middle class, the Enlightenment, and the subsequent revolutions in Europe and America. And these, in turn, influenced the thoughts and deeds of Stanton and Douglass.

Luther's theological fight in the Church toppled, or at least radically redefined, the unspoken spiritual authority of the time, and helped to establish a new spiritual locus, or "rock bottom," Erikson's term for the ultimate, stark point where the old crashes and a new, revolutionary, "ideological promise" is born. By addressing the shared experience of untold other unhappy Catholics, Luther's "solution roughly bridges a political and psychological vacuum which history had created in a significant portion of Western Christendom. Such coincidence, if further coinciding with the deployment of highly specific personal gifts, makes for historical greatness" (*Young Man Luther*, 15). I maintain that the deed of Stanton and Douglass at Seneca Falls makes it possible for us to bridge the political, psychological, and spiritual vacuum in American society by providing the ideological promise for a new American revolution.

Erikson's speculations about an ideological promise for modern times that might have the same gravity as that initiated by Luther seem to support this assertion. The new liturgy for him is the unity of the human race. With one human species, and one common technology, history is primed for a change. "The question is: Will mankind realize that it is one species — or is it destined to remain divided into 'pseudo-species' forever playing out one (necessarily incomplete) version of mankind against all others" (*Life History*, 47). Indeed, "[O]nly a new biocultural history (created by women and men articulately self-observing and communicative) could clarify the evolution of the masochistic potential in our man-made world, and of our overadjustment to it" (241–42).

Thus, as his new ideology, Erikson chooses that of a "specieshood" — that is, global unity, cooperation between men and women, and an ethic to manage a technology that, if left to its own devices, is destructive and not in service to any set of guiding, moral principles. For such a historical change to become possible in America, however, America must first resolve its own identity crisis, brought on by the social, psychological, and spiritual vacuum of the times and the multiplicity of identities, including those of men and women, black and white, clamoring for recognition.

The historical significance of the American nation turns on this question of American identity. For America's "historical moment" — to use Erikson's term for the convergence of crisis, rock bottom, and destiny — is centered on the question of acquiring identity in a diverse society, just as the historical moment of Germany in the early 1500s centered on the question of a new religious identity. And, although American culture behaves as if no such historically defining moment had occurred, I believe it has. I believe that a challenge equal in importance to Luther's was issued in the Wesleyan Chapel in Seneca Falls. I believe that if we are to find our way through a fractured national experience, divided over race, gender and religion, we must take up that fight.

Douglass and Stanton fundamentally destabilized America's spiritual locus and thereby became the twin moral equivalents of Martin Luther. Entering history at a necessary and difficult time, the two stood together at rock bottom and posted their challenge, in essence, right on the door of the American Christian establishment that prohibited the equality of women and winked at the institution of slavery. By this deed, they created a new American paradigm and earned the authority and the symbolic tools to ceremonialize the soul and initiate our country in the name of a reconstituted spiritual center.

Erikson stipulates that to search for identity an individual must "give in to some of his most regressed or repressed tendencies in order, as it were, to test rock bottom and to recover some of his as yet undeveloped childhood strengths. This, however, is safe only where a relatively stable society provides collective experiences of a ceremonial character, or where revolutionary leaders (such as Luther) provide new identity guidelines which permit the adolescent individual to take chances with himself" (*Life History,* 22).

In their collaboration, Stanton and Douglass provide that revolutionized center from which the work of identity achievement in America can now be ceremonialized. But, to explore further the rock bottom of a generalized American initiation into adulthood, we must dig even deeper in time and refer to anthropologists like E. I. Eisenstadt and Arnold Van Gennep, who have studied ancient rites of passage the world over.

Eisenstadt explains industrial society as a dislocation between history and myth, or as he refers to it, between linear and cosmic time, which he says has been especially harmful to children. "The close linkage between the growth of personality, psychological maturation, and definite role models derived from the adult world has become greatly weakened. Hence the very coalescence of youth into special groups only tends to emphasize their problematic, uncertain standing from the point of view of cultural values and symbols" ("Archetypal Patterns of Youth," 33).

Eisenstadt outlines the ancient ceremonies of transition by which adolescents were for centuries transformed into full members of a tribe, always within a religious or magical framework that provided a link to the cosmos. Although fragments of these ceremonies jam the museums of the world, the ceremonies themselves are now missing as living, formalized rites of passage in our fragmented industrial society. In our time, this mystery has succumbed to bureaucracy. To understand such fragments, with Eisenstadt's help, makes it possible to recombine them in an effort to build again a sacred, initiatory context for a worthy contemporary ideological promise.

It should come as no surprise that one of the elements of this ancient initiatory process is a "fight" in sacred precincts, the "dramatization of the encounter between several generations, a dramatization that may take the form of a fight or a competition" (27). Such a fight is part of the ritual process, of the old giving way to the new.

Van Gennep's study of rites of passage suggests that even the territorial frontier between two communities or two peoples can become a threshold, so to speak, and also the occasion for a sacred rite of passage. To cross such a threshold "is to unite oneself with new life" (*Rites of Passage*, 9). The frontiers between men and women, between black and white, between one ideological or psychosocial promise and another, constitute a threshold, the occasion for a sacred rite of passage. But without consciousness of the fight — the challenge — that took place in the church in Seneca Falls, our age is still without any reference to sacred and paradoxical frontiers and thresholds that might provide the ground for a true psychosocial initiation. American freedom has been based on a confusion of frontiers, and therefore its initiations have been erroneous.

Furthermore, Van Gennep writes, "It seems . . . likely that one dimension of mental illness may arise because an increasing number of individuals are forced to accomplish their transition alone and with private symbols" (xvi). In America, understanding mental illness, as well as achieving identity, pivot on the spiritual and cultural reorientation to the new ideological promise of "specieshood," which Erikson foresees and which Douglass and Stanton personify.

"Personifying" is James Hillman's word for attributing feelings and experiences to the actions of mythic figures. He says this is exactly what Freud did by imagining the primal horde and by using the Oedipal situation as a mythic vehicle for understanding what are essentially hidden processes of the soul. What is more, Hillman specifically draws attention to the feminine, saying that the tradition in Western civilization has been to push aside what is contained there — that is, depth, darkness, feeling, love, imagination. He says that traditional psychology has lost its feminine soul, its "psyche," once schooled by religion and myth, and warns that we are now stranded amid the sterile instrumentalities of science without a clue how to see through the names of sickness to the faces of healing gods. "Rather than a field of forces, we are each a field of internal personal relationships, an interior commune, a body politic. Psychodynamics becomes psychodramatics; our life is less the resultant of pressures and forces than the enactment of mythical scenarios" (*Revisioning Psychology,* 22). Therefore Hillman calls for healing to be based in the imaginal and feminine soul, which requires "an epistemology of the heart, a thought mode of feeling" that "we do wrong to judge . . . as inferior, archaic thinking appropriate only to those allowed emotive speech and affective logic — children, madmen, poets, and primitives."

Hillman, at the very least, seeks those images and symbols that carry the imagination of our age, and that can not be carried by modern psychology alone. Echoing Tillich, he says our important work lies on a "vertical dimension between what is above and what is below, a reflection in imaginal geography of our cultural history" (223). He thus points us south and down, toward the feminine soul. We must look there first of all for the psychological and spiritual ceremony of initiation that we need — there, in its depths — and then we must seek the corresponding formulations to the north; and, finally, we must find a path between them that would light up the inhering soul.

The Seneca Falls ceremony suggests at the very least that boys and girls must learn to borrow attributes from the opposite sex in order to come into their full personhood, to become whole men and women. In other words, boys must go south, that is, into their depth, where the feminine soul resides, while girls must go north, where the traditionally masculine intellect lives. This is not new. It just has not been psychologized, or ceremonialized — that is, sacralized. This, the events of Seneca Falls now authorize us to do.

And Stanton has given us some specific directions for the journey, as Carol Gilligan points out in *In a Different Voice*, stressing "Stanton's boldness in telling a reporter to 'put it down in capital letters: SELF-DEVELOPMENT IS A HIGHER DUTY THAN SELF-SACRIFICE. The thing which most retards and militates against women's self-development is self-sacrifice'" (quoted in Gilligan, 129). The path that begins in the feminist, imaginal, and mythic potential of the Woman's Rights Convention, centered in the lives of Elizabeth Cady Stanton and Frederick Douglass, leads males and females alike, to the moral, spiritual, and cultural redemption we yearn to experience.

Divergent as they are professionally, Erikson, Gilligan, and Hillman can become initiating elders in a line of authority that goes back to Stanton and Douglass; their sacred task to help effect an American conversion for both individuals and groups in a new age.

Consciousness of the events of Seneca Falls, then, modulates the psychosocial maturation process of boys and girls, north and south, in the name of Erikson's one "specieshood." The events ceremonialize the fight in initiatory, sacred space to which Eisenstadt refers, reconnecting history and myth, linear and cosmic time. The Seneca Falls Convention embodies public symbols of transition that guide us across the dangerous thresholds between races and sexes. It personifies Hillman's notion of the transformative "mythical scenario," anchored as it is in the deep feminine, ceremonializing the coming of age of America. As "psychodramatics," in fact, it becomes the equivalent, in our post-modern age, of Freud's Oedipus myth.

The total, faith-generating and soul-making power of arriving in Seneca Falls explains why I became a member of the Bahá'í Faith, which I did in the 1970s in Portland, Maine — a radical decision in Tillich's terms. And where Tillich illuminates an individual's spiritual space, and Erikson, Gilligan, and Hillman, in effect, ceremonialize it, for me the Bahá'í Faith constructs a dynamic house of worship on the fulminating spiritual and social center of America itself, to which the deeds of Douglass and Stanton are absolutely intrinsic. My becoming a Bahá'í was in part a protest against the "northern consciousness," the dominantly secular and mechanistic way of knowing of Western civilization. It oriented me to my own depth, height, and inner space and led me backward and forward to the meaning of Seneca Falls.

The Bahá'í Faith can be understood as Erikson's contemporary ideological promise writ large. It teaches the unity of all peoples, all races, and the equality of men and women. It holds that the earth is presently experiencing the destruction of the old order rooted in a science now run amok, the mutually exclusive sovereignty of nation states, and the horrific clash of superstition, power imbalances, and prejudice of all kinds. But, as the breakdown of the old order accelerates, the Bahá'í Faith asserts that a subtle, creative, and soul-animated process will emerge that will ultimately provide a just basis for the uniting of the human race in a federation of nations and for a harmonious technology subservient to a rejuvenated moral sense. It embodies rites of passage for the individual within a multicultural context. It can thus be seen as a sort of global waterworks for channelling underground soul and renewing world civilization. Goulds Pumps gone God.

In an interesting parallel to the events in Seneca Falls, it was another fight in a church in July 1848 that dramatically defined the emergence of the Bahá'í Faith, although in this case the fight took place in a tent. The Herald of the Bahá'í Faith, known as the Báb or Gate, claimed to be the Primal Point between the Adamic Cycle then ending, and the newly inaugurated Bahá'í Cycle. During the tumult that followed such a spectacular claim in a country that understands Muhammed to be the Seal of the Prophets, the followers of the Báb, known as Bábís, were much persecuted. The Báb himself was imprisoned several times and finally executed. To declare their independence from Islam, certain of the Báb's followers called a conference in July 1848 on the plains of Bada<u>sh</u>t, in the Iranian Province of <u>Kh</u>urasan. One Bahá'í historian states, "On every day of that memorable gathering a law or a tradition of Islam was abrogated, followed by lively discussion among these able and articulate men and the few women" (quoted in Ruhe, 86).

Present at Bada<u>sh</u>t was one of the Báb's most influential followers, a woman known as Táhirih, a poet. In a large tent set up for the conference, Táhirih stood before a group of men who, while attracted to the Bábí Movement, were also to some extent still steeped in traditional Islam. To the horrified gasps of most of those present, Táhirih unveiled herself and exclaimed, "This day is the day of festivity and universal rejoicing, the day on which the fetters of the past are burst asunder. Let those who have shared in this great achievement arise and embrace each other" (quoted in Ruhe, 88). Today, we can only dimly imagine the audacity of her act, but one man in the audience slit his throat in a gesture of horror (although it is said that he eventually recovered).

Táhirih was finally arrested in 1852 by the cleric-driven Iranian government; she was killed by military guards and thrown down an abandoned well. Her words to her executioner before he casually strangled her were, "You can kill me as soon as you like, but you cannot stop the emancipation of women" (quoted in Ruhe, 151). A moment before, she had offered the guards one of her own scarves for their murderous deed.

Táhirih's act of supreme blasphemy in a Muslim society, that required women to be veiled and wholly submissive, was a decisive deed of the Badasht conference and opened the way to the development of the world-embracing Bahá'í Faith, inaugurated in 1863 by Bahá'u'lláh, whom the Báb had heralded. Hence Bahá'ís are followers of Bahá'u'lláh.

The Bahá'í Faith claims to be the most recent in an ancient, cyclical, divine process of God's covenanting with humankind. And for the first time in history, that covenant is explicitly intended for the entire human race, men and women, and not just for a particular nationality, class, race, or region of the world.

In addition to the equality of men and women and the oneness of the human race, the distinguishing principles of Bahá'í polity include the independent search after truth, the fundamental unity of all religions, the condemnation of all forms of prejudice, the recognition of the harmony which underlies religion and science, the abolition of the extremes of wealth and poverty, the institution of a world tribunal for the adjudication of disputes, and the glorification of justice as the governing principle in human affairs. Bahá'u'lláh, born in Iran in 1817 (d. 1892), introduced these teachings when such concepts were not only anathema but even incomprehensible to parochial clerics.

The Bahá'ís would say that the spiritual teachings of all religions agree, but the social teachings of each succeeding dispensation have been incremental, leading to increasingly more complex loyalties, from family to tribe to nation, and now to the community of the world, based on the equal footing of men and women and the belief that all human beings are "leaves of one tree," with God at center. To hold this ideal up in America, where the white and black elements of the population are so seemingly divergent, and where feminism still fights for its life, is to be, bravely, a resident of Seneca Falls.

I found humility in the Bahá'í Faith. It gave me a measure of distances in relation to center, as well as a perspective on the wobble in my personal life. I felt true ecstasy. I had arrived at the river that separates but also connects. I loved my way across. My wife held my hand for much of the way because she, also a Bahá'í, was the stronger swimmer.

This was an initiation, a rite of passage. Today, we are all called upon to haul, in a wobbly ox-cart if necessary, the essential pioneering things of faith and a personal identity that integrates masculine and feminine sensibilities within sacred precincts. Human beings today are called to become religious in this deepest sense. Tillich says, "He who enters the sphere of faith enters the sanctuary of life" *(Dynamics,* 12). To arrive in Seneca Falls is to enter such a sanctuary, a house of worship indeed, the memorializable center of the American soul. It is there, within the compass of holy combat, that we find the sacred rites of our nation, its psychological and spiritual reformation.

CHAPTER SEVENTEEN

Returning to Seneca Falls:
Shaseonce

The present day village of Seneca Falls can be found on any map of New York State. It is a small village of approximately 8,000 inhabitants, at the downward apex of a triangle formed with Syracuse about forty-five miles to the northeast and Rochester about fifty miles to the northwest. Seneca Falls sits at the northern tip of Cayuga Lake, with Ithaca at the southern end. Geneva is about ten miles to the west, at the northern end of Seneca Lake, Auburn about fifteen miles to the east. The village is sliced by U.S. routes 5 and 20 and lies along the New York State Thruway at exit 41.

One nineteenth-century observer of Seneca Falls, Mr. David Lum, claimed he

> . . . if not the first to settle at Seneca Falls was intimately acquainted with those who were, and with those who were the first to feast their eyes on the wild scenery of the Shaseonce, the "swift or rolling water" of the Seneca outlet, as it dashed and leaped from rock to rock in foaming beauty among the little islands, of which there were several in these rapids, rushing past the tangled mass of forest on its banks like the jugular current of some mighty monster. (1)

Lum tells us:

> The army under Gen. Sullivan in 1779 had destroyed the power of the Indians and the war of the revolution had brought peace to the frontiers and safety to the pioneers in their efforts to penetrate and subdue this primitive [sic] wilderness. . . . Missionaries had undoubtedly been extensively scattered through this

whole land for many years before the revolutionary war, but they, with white prisoners and white traders among the Indians, did not constitute a government or a settlement. They were only path-finders. It sometimes happened that when a permanent settler came to locate in these wilds he would find one of these pathfinders there before him. (1–2)

For me, Seneca Falls is just as much a place of the imagination as it is a modest village in upstate New York, and because of the events of 1848 it is still situated on the frontiers of civilization. In this sense, Shaseonce is perhaps one of the most daunting locales in America, fortified by all manner of prejudice and fear, and all forms of tradition and taboo that carry the sanctimonious stamp of approval by assorted priests, bluebloods, and so-called pillars of the community. In fact, the majority of Americans, who otherwise may be intelligent, generous and charitable, are nevertheless still unprepared or ignorant or downright fearful of that place of the heart where women ascend and black people take their rightful places in personhood and community. As we know, the impact of the events of Seneca Falls has not yet been fully felt in modern society. To the extent that women are still regarded as sexual objects and black people still as invisible, the events of Seneca Falls are dead history and not living myth. Shaseonce, the place of breakthrough, represents the integration of whatever lies scattered, misunderstood, chained up, and feared in the shadows of our unconscious, now rearranged into a more aerodynamic soul capable of carrying us into the twenty-first century and beyond.

Listen to David Lum:

> Adventurous settlers were penetrating the unbroken forests guided by the blased [sic] trees to the corners of lots, the numbers on which would indicate to them the place of their future abode. Thus here and there, miles apart, without roads, were found emphatically the first families in this country, and it must be admitted that they were a gamey set of men . . . they undoubtedly did a good deal of shooting, there being abundant supply of bear, wolves, deer and other animals at hand. But the

flutter of the first waterwheel had not as yet been heard to mingle its monotone with the music of the dancing waters at Seneca
Falls. (3)

There are still pathfinders at this very moment exploring
for it, for the soul-center of America, where, if they could
make pilgrimage, they could recreate themselves. Shaseonce
is the sacred center of America, and, as the Lakota holy man
Black Elk taught, the center can be anywhere. Hearty men
and women, "adventurous settlers," who realize that we
human beings are far from finished yet in our personal, evo-
lutionary work, are right now out scouting for the coordi-
nates of Shaseonce, without roads, miles apart from one
another, guided by faint blazes on trees and the distant sound
of "dancing waters."

Every time I pick up progressive contemporary magazines,
I find at least one article that explores race, gender, our treat-
ment of the environment, or the state of feminism. Many
bright and able people are vigorously searching for a method,
a metaphor, a moral map that would point them in the direction of the new world so that they could get their bearings
in this disorienting time.

For men, the longitudes and latitudes that locate the center of Shaseonce are genuine love for women, commitment to
work, willingness to fight, and participation in the ecological and human web of community. The spiritual energy of
manhood communicates back and forth along the lines of
these main force fields and emerges like branches from the
cross-section of self, forming not an overweening Christian
cross of suffering but an irrepressible tree of life. Men are
mini-trees that maintain relationship with the literal earth
and sky as well as with the moral and soulful ground of being
and the mysterious heaven of spiritual infinity. I see it all as
a living dynamic. The thrust of the spirit, or soul, on its way
back and forth from God, through the agency of the heart
and mind, and as it manifests itself like mighty branches in
relation to the phenomenon of women, war, web, and work,

simultaneously pushes and embraces, raises questions and answers them, creates and destroys.

I explored the necessity for male approaches to women that require more wholly passionate and considerate understanding, that do not dilute the strength of male sexuality but place it in a crown with other jewels. And I have made a case for becoming warlike in a new world, with requisite strength, courage and self-sacrifice aimed at the reformation of oneself upon battlefields that are political, educational, spiritual, and artistic. I believe that as we move toward the sacred ground of Shaseonce, in the middle of the Iroquois Nation under the shadow of their traditional Great Tree of Law, we men must come to understand our relationship to the web of river, flower, ocean, and sky, and thus be more likely to enter into an enduring relationship with the organic unity of life, with men and women, with blacks, whites, reds, and yellows.

At Shaseonce we are invited to absorb the "otherness" of Elizabeth Cady Stanton and Frederick Douglass, and to trade our seemingly self-contained, isolated, and steely masked individualistic idea of who we are — we white men in particular — for community in a local, global, and ecological sense. We men cannot experience the kind of spiritual and moral revolution inherent in understanding the events of Seneca Falls without reconnecting with the feminine, without integrating our moral integrity, without sensing the Indian blood in the soil of Shaseonce, and without thereby giving birth to a sacred earth consciousness.

I have not touched on work as one of those four grandfather directions that can teach and nurture and scold on our way to becoming men. Wendell Berry, the poet, farmer, and teacher, says this about work:

> The growth of the exploiters' revolution on this continent has been accompanied by the growth of the idea that work is beneath human dignity, particularly any form of hand work. We have made it our overriding ambition to escape work, and as a

consequence have debased work until it is only fit to escape from. We have debased the products of work and have been, in turn, debased by them. . . .

But is work something that we have a right to escape? And can we escape it with impunity? We are probably the first entire people ever to think so. All the ancient wisdom that has come down to us counsels us otherwise. It tells us that work is necessary to us, as much a part of our condition as mortality; that good work is our salvation and our joy; that shoddy or dishonest or self-serving work is our curse and our doom. We have tried to escape the sweat and sorrow promised in Genesis — only to find that, in order to do so, we must foreswear love and excellence, health and joy. (12)

Likewise, the nineteenth-century Seneca Falls observer Henry Stowell says:

It will be an evil day, full of sad and bitter results, when labor shall fail to command the respect of the people, and laboring men be degraded on account of their labor. True republicanism regards the equality of men, and admits that beneath all the rags and ribbons of accidental condition there is the human soul, with all its God-given powers, and within the breast of the dust-covered and toil-worn, there beats the true heart of manhood, working out its destiny and directing its course for the achievements of time and eternity. (2)

If thanksgiving is the word for the appropriate attitude toward a bountiful land and a mysterious God, then work is the operative word for relationships to them. It was the help the Pilgrims received from Squanto and the Wampanoags, and the courage to put their collective pilgrim shoulders to the work of this relatively unknown continent, that enabled them, for better or worse, to crack the code of the New World. Maybe our world would have been more humane if the Pilgrims and subsequent Europeans had failed to survive on this forbidding continent and the Indians had not succumbed by the hundreds of thousands to white men's diseases. Surely the Indian nations would have fared better. But to so speculate is absurd, and many of us, like it or not, are the children of Pilgrim fathers.

The Pilgrims landed in December at what was then named Plymouth, exhausted, some suffering from scurvy and pneumonia, with limited supplies of hardtack and pickled meat. The men and boys first labored in freezing weather to hew timber and then build a Common House that served as a hospital and sleeping area. The girls and women lived primarily on the Mayflower that first winter, moored about one and a half miles off shore. As the first spring arrived, of the original one hundred and two passengers, half had died; entire families were obliterated, and after that first winter half the colony was composed of children sixteen years old or younger. Hardly a family was spared at least one death during the winter. Only four mothers were left alive.

Squanto, a member of the disease-desiccated tribe that once lived at the site where the Pilgrims were then homesteading, guided the separatists through the ensuing months with expert advice on planting procedures, baking clams and mussels, trapping fish and deer, preparing eels, scorching corn for storage, gathering cranberries. Squanto showed the Pilgrims how to work intelligently here. During the spring the Pilgrims managed to build seven houses and three more public buildings.

We have understood that only by applying some kind of spiritually intelligent, feminine-informed force against the apparent resistance of earth, of steel, of ideas, can a new, creative entity be born.

Sam Keen has written:

The way forward for moderns . . . begins when men and women hear and respond to a common vocation to come together to create a new kind of social order that is not based upon emnity and the hope of conquest. . . .

And, as part and parcel of the same vocation, we must take on the enormous century-long project of changing the style of political and general relationships that keep the warfare system alive and deadly. . . .

It falls to men and women today to begin a journey. As it was at the beginning of every pivotal era in human history, so it is in ours. . . . As prodigal sons and daughters all we know is that we must leave the father's household, as we once left the mother's, and travel into a strange country. Perhaps along the way, if we make common cause, we may become true companions. (231–232)

So it is to the wayfarers that I address myself, the travelers in search of Shaseonce, "hearty men and women," a gamey set who are guided by faint blazes and who listen for "dancing waters." Having myself departed certain boundaries of love and heroism and acquired a new self based on the mythological examples of Stanton and Douglass, I now turn and return always in reference to the soul-center of Seneca Falls. I spin like a turbine on fire, forever generating sparks upon the dry, flat lands lying beyond the circle that defines the events of this historic hamlet.

Having met its heroes and forged in its industrial ambience a crude character fountain of unity within, I am now a kind of assistant to fellow wayfarers, an unkempt Job Smith who hides from the authorities in among the Indians, helping pathfinders across the rapids. In my wagon hauled by the force of oxen and floated on circles of sawed logs, I lash together a simple bundle of male and female, black and white. I retain knowledge of local and historical moment that others have forgotten. I work daily at the task of restoring the lines of communication between this side and that, between the conscious and unconscious zones of the human psyche. I have overcome inertia. It is now my responsiblity to define Shaseonce further, to define the very circle that indwells like circulating blood in the soil of all of America. This is my work, in Campbell's sense, my return.

Declaration of Rights and Sentiments

*Adopted by the
Seneca Falls Convention
July 19–20, 1848*

When in the course of human events it becomes necessary for one portion of the family of man to assume among the people of the earth a position different from that which the laws of nature and of nature's God entitle them, a decent respect to the opinions of mankind requires that they should declare the causes that impel them to such a course.

We hold these truths to be self-evident; that all men and women are created equal; that they are endowed by their Creator with certain inalienable rights; that among these are life, liberty, and the pursuit of happiness; that to secure these rights governments are instituted, deriving their just powers from the consent of the governed. Whenever any form of government becomes destructive of these ends, it is the right of those who suffer from it to refuse allegiance to it, and to insist upon the institution of a new government, laying its foundation on such principles, and organizing its powers in such form as to them shall seem most likely to effect their safety and happiness. Prudence, indeed, will dictate that governments long established should not be changed for light and transient causes; and accordingly, all experience hath shown that mankind are more disposed to suffer, while evils are sufferable, than to right themselves by abolishing the forms to which they are accustomed. But when a long train of abuses and usurpation, pursuing invariably the same object, evinces a design to reduce them under absolute despotism, it is their duty to throw off such government, and to provide new guards for their future security. Such has been the patient sufferance of the women under this government, and such is now the necessity which constrains them to demand the equal station to which they are entitled.

The history of mankind is a history of repeated injuries and usurpation on the part of man toward woman, having in direct object the establishment of an absolute tyranny over her. To prove this, let facts be submitted to a candid world.

He has never permitted her to exercise her inalienable right to the elective franchise.

He has compelled her to submit to laws, in the formation of which she has no voice.

He has withheld from her rights which are given to the most ignorant and degraded men — both natives and foreigners.

Having deprived her of this first right of a citizen, the elective franchise, thereby leaving her without representation in the halls of legislation, he has oppressed her on all sides.

He has made her, if married, in the eye of the law, civilly dead.

He has taken from her all right in property, even to the wages she earns.

He has made her, morally, an irresponsible being, as she can commit many crimes with impunity, provided they be done in the presence of her husband. In the covenant of marriage, she is compelled to promise obedience to her husband, he becoming, to all intents and purposes, her master — the law giving him power to deprive her of liberty, and to administer chastisements.

He has so framed the laws of divorce, as to what shall be the proper causes of divorce; in case of separation, to whom the guardianship of the children shall be given; as to be wholly regardless of the happiness of women — the law, in all cases, going upon the false supposition of the supremacy of man, and giving all powers into his hands.

After depriving her of all rights as a married woman, if single and the owner of property, he has taxed her to support a government which recognizes her only when her property can be made profitable to it.

He has monopolized nearly all the profitable employments, and from those she is permitted to follow, she receives but a scanty remuneration.

He closes against her all the avenues to wealth and distinction, which he considers most honorable to himself. As a teacher of theology, medicine, or law, she is not known.

He has denied her the facilities for obtaining a thorough education, all colleges being closed against her.

He allows her in Church, as well as State, but a subordinate position, claiming Apostolic authority for her exclusion from the ministry, and, with some exceptions, from any public participation in the affairs of the Church.

He has created a false public sentiment, by giving to the world a different code of morals for men and women, by which moral delinquencies which exclude women from society, are not only tolerated but deemed of little account in man.

He has usurped the prerogative of Jehovah himself, claiming it as his right to assign for her a sphere of action, when that belongs to her conscience and her God.

He has endeavored, in every way that he could to destroy her confidence in her own powers, to lessen her self-respect, and to make her willing to lead a dependent and abject life.

Now, in view of this entire disfranchisement of one-half the people of this country, their social and religious degradation — in view of the unjust laws above mentioned, and because women do feel themselves aggrieved, oppressed, and fraudulently deprived of their most sacred rights, we insist that they have immediate admission to all the rights and privileges which belong to them as citizens of these United States.

In entering upon the great work before us, we anticipate no small amount of misconception, misrepresentation, and ridicule; but we shall use every instrumentality within our power to effect our object. We shall employ agents, circulate tracts, petition the State and national Legislatures, and endeavor to enlist the pulpit and the press in our behalf. We hope this Convention will be followed by a series of Conventions embracing every part of the country. (Gurko 307–9)

≈⊚≈

Resolutions Presented at the Seneca Falls Convention

Whereas, The great precept of nature is conceded to be, that "man shall pursue his own true and substantial happiness." Blackstone in his commentaries remarks[1] that this law of Nature being coeval with mankind, and dictated by God himself, is of course superior in obligation to any other. It is binding over all the globe, in all countries and at all times; no human laws are of any validity if contrary to this, and such of them as are valid, derive all their force, and all their validity, and all their authority, mediately and immediately from this original; therefore,

RESOLVED, That such laws as conflict, in any way, with the true and substantial happiness of woman, are contrary to the great precept of Nature, and of no validity, for this is "superior in obligation to any other."

RESOLVED, That all laws which prevent woman from occupying such a station in society as her conscience shall dictate, or which place her in a position inferior to that of man, are contrary to the great precept of Nature and therefore of no force or authority.

---

[1] [Blackstone's *Commentaries on the Laws of England,* which appeared first in 1765-69, codified the view that women had no legal, public existence: "By marriage, the husband and wife are one person in law: that is, the very being or legal existence of the woman is suspended during marriage, or at least is incorporated and consolidated into that of the husband: under whose wing, protection, and cover she performs everything. . ." (Donovan 4).]

RESOLVED, That woman is man's equal — was intended to be so by her Creator, and the highest good of the race demands that she should be recognized as such.

RESOLVED, That the women of this country ought to be enlightened with regard to the laws under which they live, that they may no longer publish their degradation by declaring themselves satisfied with their present position, nor their ignorance, by asserting they have all the rights they want.

RESOLVED, That inasmuch as man, while claiming for himself intellectual superiority, does accord to woman moral superiority, it is pre-eminently his duty to encourage her to speak and teach as she has opportunity, in all religious assemblies.

RESOLVED, That the same amount of virtue, delicacy, and refinement of behavior that is required of woman in the social state, should also be required of man, and the same transgressions should be visited with equal severity on both man and woman.

RESOLVED, That the objection of indelicacy and impropriety which is so often brought against woman when she addresses a public audience, comes with very ill grace from those who encourage, by their attendance, her appearance on the stage, in the concert, or in feats of the circus.

RESOLVED, That woman has too long rested satisfied in the circumscribed limits which corrupt customs and a perverted application of the Scriptures have marked out for her, and that it is time she should move in the enlarged sphere which her great Creator has assigned her.

RESOLVED, That it is the duty of the women of this country to secure to themselves their sacred right to the elective franchise.

RESOLVED, That the equality of human rights results necessarily from the fact of the identity of the race in capabilities and responsibilities.

RESOLVED, therefore, That being invested by the Creator with the same capabilities, and the same consciousness of responsibility for their exercise, it is demonstrably the right and duty of woman, equally with man, to promote every righteous cause by every righteous means; and especially in regard to the great subjects of morals and religion, it is self-evidently her right to participate with her brother in teaching them, both in private and in public, by writing and by speaking, by any instrumentalities proper be used, and in any assemblies proper to be held; and this being a self-evident truth growing out of the divinely implanted principles of human nature, any custom or authority adverse to it, whether modern or wearing the hoary sanction of antiquity, is to be regarded as self-evident falsehood, and at war with mankind. (Gurko, 309–11)

APPENDIX THREE

~~≈✿≋~~

Elizabeth Cady Stanton's 1848 Seneca Falls Woman's Rights Convention Speech *(abridged)*

I should feel exceedingly diffident to appear before you at this time, having never before spoken in public, were I not nerved by a sense of right and duty, did I not feel the time had fully come for the question of woman's wrongs to be laid before the public, did I not believe that woman herself must do this work; for woman alone can understand the height, the depth, the length, and the breadth of her own degradation. Man can not speak for her. . . .

Among the many important questions which have been brought before the public, there is none that more vitally affects the whole human family than that which is technically called Woman's Rights. Every allusion to the degraded and inferior position occupied by women all over the world has been met by scorn and abuse. From the man of highest mental cultivation to the most degraded wretch who staggers in the streets do we meet ridicule, and coarse jests, freely bestowed upon those who dare assert that woman stands by the side of man, his equal, placed here by her God, to enjoy with him the beautiful earth, which is her home as it is his, having the same sense of right and wrong, and looking to the same Being for guidance and support. So long has man exercised tyranny over her, injurious to himself and numbing to his faculties, that few can nerve themselves to meet the storm; and so long has the chain been about her that she knows not there is a remedy. . . .

. . . In every country and clime does man assume the responsibility of marking out the path for her to tread. In every country does he regard her as a being inferior to himself, and one whom he is to guide and control. From the Arabian Kerek, whose wife is obliged to steal from her husband to supply the necessities of life; from the Mahometan who forbids pigs, dogs, women and other impure animals, to enter a Mosque, and does not allow a fool, madman or woman to proclaim the hour of prayer; from the German who complacently smokes his meerschaum, while his wife, yoked with the ox, draws the plough through its furrow; from the delectable carpet-knight, who thinks an inferior style of conversation adapted to woman; to the legislator, who considers her incapable of saying what laws shall govern her, is the same feeling manifested. . . .

Let us consider . . . man's superiority, intellectually, morally, physically.

Man's intellectual superiority cannot be a question until woman has had a fair trial. When we shall have had our freedom to find out our sphere, when we shall have had our colleges, our professions, our trades, for a century, a comparison then may be justly instituted. When woman, instead of being taxed to endow colleges where she is forbidden to enter — instead of forming sewing societies to educate 'poor, but pious,' young men, shall first educate herself, when she shall be just to herself before she is generous to others; improving the talents God has given her, and leaving her neighbor to do the same for himself, we shall not hear so much about this boasted superiority. . . .

In consideration of man's moral superiority, glance now at our theological seminaries, our divinity students, the long line of descendents from our Apostolic fathers, the immaculate priesthood, and what do we find there? Perfect moral rectitude in every relation of life, a devoted spirit of self-sacrifice, a perfect union of thought, opinion, and feeling among those who profess to worship God, and whose laws they feel themselves called upon to declare to a fallen race? Far from it. . . . Is the moral and religious life of this class what we might expect from minds said to be fixed on mighty themes? By no means. . . . The lamentable want of principle among our lawyers, generally, is too well known to need comment. The everlasting backbiting and bickering of our physicians is proverbial. The disgraceful riots at our polls, where man, in performing the highest duty of citizenship, ought surely to be sober-minded, the perfect rowdyism that now characterizes the debates in our national Congress, — all these are great facts which rise up against man's claim for moral superiority. In my opinion, he is infinitely woman's inferior in every moral quality, not by nature, but made so by a false education. . . .

. . . God's commands rest upon man as well as woman. It is as much his duty to be kind, self-denying and full of good works, as it is hers. As much his duty to absent himself from scenes of violence as it is hers. A place or position that would require the sacrifice of the delicacy and refinement of woman's nature is unfit for man, for these virtues should be as carefully guarded in him as in her. . . . I would not have woman less pure, but I would have men more so. I would have the same code of morals for both. . . .

Let us now consider man's claim to physical superiority. Methinks I hear some say, surely, you will not contend for equality here. Yes, we must not give an inch, lest you take an ell. We cannot accord to man even this much, and he has no right to claim it until the fact has been fully demonstrated. . . . We cannot say what the woman might be physically, if the girl were allowed all the freedom of the boy in romping, climbing, swimming, playing whoop and ball.

Among some of the Tartar tribes of the present day, women manage a horse, hurl a javelin, hunt wild animals and fight an enemy as well as a man. The Indian women endure fatigues and carry burdens that some of our fair-faced, soft-handed, moustached young gentlemen would consider quite impossible for them to sustain. . . .

But there is a class of objectors who say they do not claim superiority, they merely assert a difference. But you will find by following them up closely, that they soon run this difference into the old groove of superiority. . . .

We have met here today to discuss our rights and wrongs, civil and political, and not, as some have supposed, go into the detail of social life alone. We do not propose to petition the legislature to make our husbands just, generous and courteous, to seat every man at the head of a cradle, and to clothe every woman in male attire. . . .

We are assembled to protest against a form of government, existing without the consent of the governed — to declare our right to be free as man is free, to be represented in the government which we are taxed to support, to have such disgraceful laws as give man the power to chastise and imprison his wife, to take the wages which she earns, the property which she inherits, and, in the case of separation, the children of her love; laws which make her the mere dependent on his bounty. It is to protest against such unjust laws as these that we are assembled today, and to have them, if possible, forever erased from our statute-books, deeming them a shame and a disgrace to a Christian republic in the nineteenth century. . . .

And, strange as it may seem to many, we now demand our right to vote according to the declaration of the government under which we live. . . . We have no objection to discuss the question of equality, for we feel that the weight of argument lies wholly with us, but we wish the question of equality kept distinct from the question of rights, for the proof of the one does not determine the truth of the other. All white men in this country have the same rights, however they may differ in mind, body or estate. The right is ours. The question now is, how shall we get possession of what rightfully belongs to us. . . . To have drunkards, idiots, horse-racing, rumselling rowdies, ignorant foreigners, and silly boys fully recognized, while we ourselves are thrust out from all the rights that belong to citizens, it is too grossly insulting to the dignity of woman to be longer quietly submitted to. The right is ours. Have it we must. Use it we will. The pens, the tongues, the fortunes, the indomitable wills of many women are already pledged to secure this right. The great truth, that no just government can be formed without the consent of the governed, we shall echo and re-echo in the ears of the unjust judge until by continual coming we shall weary him. . . .

When women know the laws and constitutions on which they live, they will not publish their degradation by declaring themselves satisfied, nor their ignorance, by declaring they have all the rights they want. . . .

Let woman live as she should. Let her feel her accountability to her Maker. Let her know her spirit is fitted for as high a sphere as man's, and that her soul requires food as pure and exalted as his. Let her live first for God, and she will not make imperfect man an object of reverence and awe. Teach her responsibility as a being of conscience and reason, that all earthly support is weak and unstable, and that her only safe dependence is the arm of omnipotence, and that true happiness springs from duty accomplished. Thus will she learn the lesson of individual responsibility for time and eternity. That neither father, husband, brother, or son, however willing they may be, can discharge her high duties of life, or stand in her stead when called into the presence of the great searcher of Hearts at the last day. . . .

One common objection to this movement is, that if the principles of freedom and equality which we advocate were put into practice, it would destroy all harmony in the domestic circle. Here let me ask, how many truly harmonious households have we now? . . . The only happy households we now see are those in which husband and wife share equally in counsel and government. There can be no true dignity or independence where there is subordination to the absolute will of another, no happiness without freedom. Let us then have no fears that the movement will disturb what is seldom found, a truly united and happy family. . . .

There seems now to be a kind of moral stagnation in our

midst. Philanthropists have done their utmost to rouse the nation to a sense of its aims. . . . Our churches are multiplying on all sides, our missionary societies, Sunday schools, and prayer meetings and innumerable charitable and reform organizations are all in operation, but still the tide of vice is swelling, and threatens the destruction of everything. . . . Verily, the world waits the coming of some new element, some purifying power, some spirit of mercy and love. The voice of woman has been silenced in the state, the church, and the home, but man cannot fulfill his destiny alone, he cannot redeem his race unaided. . . . The world has never seen a truly great and virtuous nation, because in the degradation of woman the very fountains of life are poisoned at their source. It is vain to look for silver and gold from mines of copper and lead. It is the wise mother that has the wise son. So long as your women are slaves you may throw your colleges and churches to the winds. . . . Truly are the sins of the fathers visited upon the children to the third and fourth generation. God, in his wisdom, has so linked the whole human family together that any violence done at one end of the chain is felt throughout its length, and here, too, is the law of restoration, as in woman all have fallen, so in her elevation shall the race be recreated.

   . . . We do not expect our path to be strewn with flowers of popular applause, but over the thorns of bigotry and prejudice will be our way, and on our banners will beat the dark storm-clouds of opposition from those who have entrenched themselves behind the stormy bulwarks of custom and authority, and who have fortified their position by every means, holy and unholy. . . . (*Correspondence, Writings, Speeches*, 28–35)

"Solitude of Self"
by Elizabeth Cady Stanton

*Delivered at the annual meeting of the
National American Woman Suffrage Association in
Washington, D.C., January 1892, and also at this time
before the Congressional Judiciary Committee,
marking her last appearance before Congress:*

The point I wish plainly to bring before you on this occasion is the individuality of each human soul; our Protestant idea, the right of individual conscience and judgement; our republican idea, individual citizenship. In discussing the rights of woman, we are to consider, first, what belongs to her as an individual, in a world of her own, the arbiter of her own destiny, an imaginary Robinson Crusoe, with her woman, Friday, on a solitary island. Her rights under such circumstances are to use all her faculties for her own safety and happiness.

Secondly, if we consider her as a citizen, as a member of a great nation, she must have the same rights as all members, according to the fundamental principles of our government.

Thirdly, viewed as a woman, an equal factor in civilization, her rights and duties are still the same; individual happiness and development.

Fourthly, it is only the incidental relations of life, such as mother, wife, sister, daughter, that may involve some special duties and training. In the usual discussion in regard to woman's sphere, such men as Herbert Spencer, Frederic Harrison and Grant Allen, uniformly subordinate her rights and duties as an individual, as a citizen, as a woman, to the necessities of those incidental relations, neither of which a large class of woman may ever assume. In discussing the sphere of man, we do not decide his rights as an individual, as a citizen, as a man, by his duties as a father, a husband, a brother or son, relations he may never fill. Moreover, he would be better fitted for these very relations, and whatever special work he might choose to earn his bread, by the complete development of all his faculties as an individual.

Just so with woman. The education that will fit her to discharge the duties in the largest sphere of human usefulness will best fit her for whatever special work she may be compelled to do.

The isolation of every human soul, and the necessity of self-independence, must give each individual the right to choose his own surroundings.

The strongest reason for giving woman all the opportunities for higher education, for the full development of her faculties, forces of mind and body; for giving her the most enlarged freedom of thought and action; a complete emancipation from all forms of bondage, of custom, dependence, superstition; from all the crippling influences of fear — is the solitude and personal responsibility of her own individual life. The strongest reason why we ask for woman a voice in the government under which she lives; in the religion she is asked to believe; equality in social life, where she is the chief factor; a place in the trades and the professions, where she may earn her bread, is because of her birthright to self-sovereignty; because, as an individual, she must rely on herself. No matter how much women prefer to lean, to be protected and supported, nor how much men desire to have them do so, they must make the voyage of life alone, and for safety in an emergency, they must know something of the laws of navigation. To guide our craft, we must be captain, pilot, engineer; with chart and compass to stand at the wheel; to watch the winds and waves, and know when to take in the sail, and to read the signs in the firmament over all. It matters not whether the solitary voyager is man or woman; nature, having endowed them equally, leaves them to their own skill and judgement in the hour of danger, and, if not equal to the occasion, alike they perish.

To appreciate the importance of fitting every human soul for independent action, think for a moment of the immeasurable solitude of self. We come into the world alone, unlike all who have gone before us, we leave it alone, under circumstances peculiar to ourselves. No mortal ever will be like the soul just launched on the sea of life. There can never again be just such a combination of prenatal influences; never again just such environments as make up the infancy, youth and manhood of this one. Nature never repeats herself, and the possibilities of one human soul will never be found in another. No one has ever found two blades of ribbon grass alike, and no one will ever find two human beings alike. Seeing, then, what must be the infinite diversity in human character, we can in a measure appreciate the loss to a nation when any large class of people is uneducated and unrepresented in the government.

We ask for the complete development of every individual, first, for his own benefit and happiness. In fitting out an army, we give each soldier his own knapsack, arms, powder, his blanket, cup, knife, fork and spoon. We provide alike for all their individual necessities; then each man bears his own burden.

Again, we ask complete individual development for the general good; for the consensus of the competent on the whole round of human interests, on all questions of national life; and here each man must bear his share of the general burden. It is sad to see how soon friendless children are left to bear their own burdens, before they can analyze their feelings; before they can even tell their joys and sorrows, they are thrown on their own resources. The great lesson that nature seems to teach us at all ages is self-dependence, self-protection, self-support. What a touching instant of a child's solitude, of that hunger of the heart for love and recognition, in the case of the little girl who helped to dress a Christmas tree for the children of the family in which she served. On finding there was no present for herself, she slipped away in the darkness and spent the night in an open field sitting on a stone, and when found in the morning was weeping as if her heart would break. No mortal will ever know the thoughts that passed through the mind of that friendless child in the long hours of that cold night, with only the silent stars to keep her company. The mention of her case in the daily papers moved many generous hearts to send her presents, but in the hours of her keenest suffering she was thrown wholly on herself for consolation.

In youth our most bitter disappointments, our brightest hopes and ambitions, are known only to ourselves. Even our friendship and love we never fully share with another; there is something of every passion, in every situation, we conceal. Even so in our triumphs and our defeats. The successful candidate for the presidency, and his opponent, each has a solitude peculiarly his own, and good form forbids either to speak of his pleasure or regret. The solitude of the king on his throne and the prisoner in his cell differs in character and degree, but it is solitude, nevertheless.

We ask no sympathy from others in the anxiety and agony of a broken friendship or shattered love. When death sunders our nearest ties, alone we sit in the shadow of our affliction. Alike amid the greatest triumphs and darkest tragedies of life, we walk alone. In the divine heights of human attainment, eulogized and worshipped as a hero or saint, we stand alone. In ignorance, poverty and vice, as a pauper or criminal, alone we starve or steal; alone we suffer the sneers and rebuffs of our fellows; alone we are hunted and hounded through dark courts and alleys, in byways and highways; alone we stand in the judgement seat; alone in the prison cell we lament our crimes and misfortunes; alone we expiate them on the gallows. In hours like these we realize the awful solitude of individual life, its pains, its penalties, its responsibilities; hours in which the youngest and the most helpless are thrown on their own resources for guidance and consolation. Seeing, then, that life must ever be a march and a battle, that each soldier must be equipped for his own protection, it is the height of cruelty to rob the individual of a single natural right.

To throw obstacles in the way of a complete education is like putting out the eyes; to deny the rights of property, like cutting off the hands. To deny political equality is to rob the ostracized of all self-respect; of credit in the market place; of recompense in the world of work; of a voice in those who make and administer the law; a choice in the jury before whom they are tried; and in the judge who decides their punishment. Shakespeare's play of TITUS ANDRONICUS contains a terrible satire on woman's position in the 19th century. Rude men (the play tells us) seized the king's daughter, cut out her tongue, cut off her hands, and then bade her go call for water and wash her hands. What a picture of woman's position! Robbed of her natural rights, handicapped by law and custom at every turn, yet compelled to fight her own battles, and in the emergencies of life to fall back on herself for protection.

A girl of sixteen, thrown on the world to support herself, to make her own place in society, to resist the temptations that surround her and maintain a spotless integrity, must do all this by native force or superior education. She does not acquire this power by being trained to trust others and distrust herself. If she wearies of the struggle, finding it hard to swim up stream, and allows herself to drift with the current, she will find plenty of company, but no one to share her misery in the hour of her deepest humiliation. If she tries to retrieve her position, to conceal the past, her life is hedged about with fears lest willing hands should tear the veil from what she fain would hide. Young and friendless, she knows the bitter solitude of self.

How the little courtesies of life on the surface of society, deemed so important from man towards woman, fade into utter insignificance in view of the deeper tragedies in which she must play her part alone, where no human aid is possible!

The young wife and mother, at the head of some establishment, with a kind husband to shield her from the adverse winds of life, with wealth, fortune and position, has a certain harbor of safety, secure against the ordinary ills of life. But to manage a household, have a desirable influence in society, keep her friends and the affections of her husband, train her children and servants well, she must have rare common sense, wisdom, diplomacy, and a knowledge of human nature. To do all of this, she needs the cardinal virtues and the strong points of character that the most successful statesman possesses. An uneducated woman trained to dependence, with no resources in herself, must make a failure of any position in life. But society says women do not need a knowledge of the world, the liberal training that experience in public life must give, all the advantages of collegiate education; but when for the lack of all this, the woman's happiness is wrecked, alone she bears her humiliation; and the solitude of the weak and the ignorant is indeed pitiable. In the wild chase for the prizes of life, they are ground to powder.

In age, when the pleasures of youth are passed, children grown up, married and gone, the hurry and bustle of life in a measure over, when the hands are weary of active service, when the old arm chair and the fireside are the chosen resorts, then men and women alike must fall back on their own resources. If they cannot find companionship in books, if they have no interest in the vital questions of the hour, no interest in watching the consummation of reforms with which they might have been identified, they soon pass into their dotage. The more fully the faculties of the mind are developed and kept in use, the longer the period of vigor and active interest in all around us continues. If, from a life-long participation in public affairs, a woman feels responsible for the laws regulating our system of education, the discipline of our jails and prisons, the sanitary conditions of our private homes, public buildings and thoroughfares, an interest in commerce, finance, our foreign relations, in any or all of these questions, her solitude will at least be respectable, and she will not be driven to gossip or scandal for entertainment.

The chief reason for opening to every soul the doors to the whole round of human duties and pleasure is the individual development thus attained, the resources thus provided under all circumstances to mitigate the solitude that at all times must come to everyone. I once asked Prince Kropotkin, a Russian Nihilist, how he endured his long years in prison, deprived of books, pen, ink and paper. "Ah!" said he, "I thought out many questions in which I had a deep interest. In the pursuit of an idea, I took no note of time. When tired of solving knotty problems, I recited all the beautiful passages in prose and verse I had ever learned. I became acquainted with myself, and my own resources. I had a world of my own, a vast empire, that no Russian jailer or Czar could invade." Such is the value of liberal thought and broad culture, when shut off from all human companionship, bringing comfort and sunshine within even the four walls of a prison cell.

As women offtimes share a similar fate, should they not have all the consolation that the most liberal education can give? Their sufferings in the prisons of St. Petersburg; in the long weary marches to Siberia, and in the mines, working side by side with men, surely call for all the self-support that the most exalted sentiments of heroism can give. When suddenly roused at midnight, with the startling cry of "Fire! Fire!" to find the house over their heads in flames, do women wait for men to point the way to safety? And are the men equally bewildered, and half suffocated with smoke, in a position to do more than try to save themselves? At such times the most timid women have shown courage and heroism, in saving their husbands and children, that has surprised everybody. Inasmuch, then, as woman shares equally the joys and sorrows of time and eternity, is it not the height of presumption in man to propose to represent her at the ballot box and the throne of grace, to do her voting in the state, her praying in the church, and to assume the position of high priest at the family altar?

Nothing strengthens the judgement and quickens the conscience like individual responsibility; nothing adds such dignity to character as the recognition of one's self-sovereignty; the right to an equal place, everywhere conceded; a place earned by personal merit, not an artificial attainment by inheritance, wealth, family and position. Seeing, then, that the responsibilities of life rest mainly on man and woman, that their destiny is the same, they need the same preparation for time and eternity. The talk of sheltering woman from the fierce storms of life is the sheerest mockery, for they beat on her from every point of the compass, just as they do on man, and with more fatal results, for he has been trained to protect himself, to resist, and to conquer. Such are the facts in human experience, the responsibilities of individual sovereignty. Rich and poor, intelligent and ignorant, wise and foolish, virtuous and vicious, man and woman; it is ever the same, each soul must depend wholly on itself.

Whatever the theories may be of woman's dependence on man, in the supreme moments of her life, he cannot bear her burdens. Alone she goes to the gates of death to give life to every man that is born into the world; no one can share her fears, no one can mitigate her pangs; and if sorrow is greater than she can bear, alone she passes beyond the gates into the vast unknown.

From the mountain-tops of Judea long ago, a heavenly voice bade his disciples, "Bear ye one another's burdens"; but humanity has not yet risen to that point of self-sacrifice; and if ever so willing, how few the burdens are that one soul can bear for another! In the highways of Palestine; in prayer and fasting on the solitary mountain-top; in the Garden of Gethsemane; before the judgement seat of Pilate; betrayed by one of his trusted disciples at his last supper; in his agonies on the cross, even Jesus of Nazareth, in those last sad days on earth, felt the awful solitude of self. Deserted by man, in agony he cries, "My God, my God, why has thou forsaken me?" And so it ever must be in the conflicting scenes of life, in the long, weary march, each one walks alone. We may have many friends, love, kindness, sympathy and charity, to smooth our pathway in everyday life, but in the tragedies and triumphs of human experience, each mortal stands alone.

But when all artificial trammels are removed, and women are recognized as individuals, responsible for their own environments, thoroughly educated for all positions in life they may be called to fill; with all the resources in themselves that liberal thought and broad culture can give; guided by their own conscience and judgement, trained to self-protection, by a healthy development of the muscular system, and skill in the use of weapons and defence; and stimulated to self-support by a knowledge of the business world and the pleasures that pecuniary independence must ever give; when women are trained in this way, they will in a measure be fitted for those hours of solitude that come alike to all, whether prepared or otherwise. As in our extremity we must depend on ourselves, the dictates of wisdom point to complete individual development.

In talking of education, how shallow the argument that each class must be educated for the special work it proposes to do, and that all those faculties not needed in this special walk (sic) must lie dormant and utterly wither for want of use, when, perhaps, these will be the very faculties needed in life's greatest energies! Some say, "Where's the use of drilling girls in the languages, the sciences, in law, medicine, theology. As wives, mothers, housekeepers, cooks, they need a different curriculum from boys who are to fill all positions. The chief cooks in our great hotels and ocean steamers are men. In our large cities, men run the bakeries; they make our bread, cake and pies. They manage the laundries; they are now considered our best milliners and dress makers. Because some men fill these departments of usefulness, shall we regulate the curriculum in Harvard and Yale to their present necessities? If not, why this talk in our best colleges of a curriculum for girls who are crowding into the trades and professions, teachers in all our public schools, rapidly filling many lucrative and honorable positions in life?

They are showing, too, their calmness and courage in the most trying hours of human experience. You have probably all read in the daily papers of the terrible storm in the Bay of Biscay, when a tidal wave made such a havoc on the shore, wrecking vessels, unroofing houses, and carrying destruction everywhere. Among other buildings, the woman's prison was demolished. Those who escaped saw men struggling to reach the shore. They promptly, by clasping hands, made a chain of themselves, and pushed out into the sea, again and again, at the risk of their lives, until they had brought six men to shore, carried them to a shelter, and done all in their power for their comfort and protection.

What special school training could have prepared these women for this sublime moment in their lives? In times like this, humanity rises above all college curriculums, and recognizes nature as the greatest of all teachers in the hour of danger and death. Women are already the equals of men in the whole realm of thought, in art, science, literature and government. With telescopic vision they explore the starry firmament and bring back the history of the planetary spheres. With chart and compass they pilot ships across the mighty deep, and with skillful fingers send electric messages around the world. In galleries of art the beauties of nature and the virtues of humanity are immortalized by them on canvas, and by their inspired touch dull blocks of marble are transformed into angels of light. In music they speak again the language of Mendelssohn, Beethoven, Chopin, Schumann, and are worthy interpreters of their great thoughts. The poetry and novels of the century are theirs, and they have touched the keynote of reform, in religion, politics and social life. They fill the editor's and professor's chair, and plead at the bar of justice; walk the wards of the hospital, and speak from the pulpit and the platform. Such is the type of womanhood that an enlightened public sentiment welcomes today, and such the triumph of the facts of life over the false theories of the past.

Is it, then, consistent to hold the developed woman of this day within the same narrow political limits as the dame with the spinning-wheel and knitting-needle occupied in the past? No! no! Machinery has taken the labors of woman, as well as man, on its tireless shoulders, the loom and the spinning-wheel are but dreams of the past; the pen, the brush, the easel, the chisel, have taken their places, while the hopes and ambitions of women are essentially changed.

We see reason sufficient in the outer conditions of human beings for individual liberty and development, but when we consider the self-dependence of every human soul we see the need of courage, judgement and the exercise of every faculty of mind and body, strengthened and developed by use, in women as well as man.

Whatever may be said of man's protecting power in ordinary conditions, amid all the terrible disasters by land and sea, in the supreme moments of danger, alone woman must ever meet the horrors of the situation. The Angel of Death even makes no royal pathway for her. Man's love and sympathy enter only into the sunshine of our lives. In that solemn solitude of self, that links us with the immeasurable and the eternal, each soul lives alone forever. A recent writer says: "I remember once, in crossing the Atlantic, to have gone upon the deck of the ship at midnight, when a dense black cloud enveloped the sky, and the great deep was roaring madly under the lashes of demoniac winds. My feeling was not of danger or fear (which is a base surrender of the immortal soul) but of utter desolation and loneliness; a little spark of life shut in by a tremendous darkness. Again I remembered to have climbed the slopes of the Swiss Alps, up beyond the point where vegetation ceases, and the stunted conifers no longer struggle against the unfeeling blasts. Around me lay a huge confusion of rocks, out of which the gigantic ice peaks shot into the measureless blue of the heavens; and again my only feeling was awful solitude!"

And yet, there is a solitude which each and every one of us has always carried with him, more inaccessible than the ice-cold mountains, more profound than the midnight sea; the solitude of self. Our inner being which we call ourself, no eye nor touch of man or angel has ever pierced. It is more hidden than the caves of the gnome; the sacred adytum of the oracle; the hidden chamber of Eleusinian mystery, for to it only omniscience is permitted to enter.

Such is individual life. Who, I ask you, can take, dare take on himself the rights, the duties, the responsibilities of another human soul? (United States Department of the Interior, "The Solitude of Self," 1–12)

꧁◉꧂

Chief Seattle's Testimony

This is a version of Chief Seattle's speech which Timothy Egan has proven to be highly fictionalized. (See Works Cited.)

The Great Chief in Washington sends word that he wishes to buy our land. The Great Chief also sends us words of friendship and good will. This is kind of him, since we know he has little need of our friendship in return. But we will consider your offer. For we know that if we do not sell, the white man may come with guns and take our land.

How can you buy or sell the sky, the warmth of the land? The idea is strange to us. If we do not own the freshness of the air and the sparkle of the water, how can you buy them?

Every part of this earth is sacred to my people.

Every shining pine needle, every sandy shore, every mist in the dark woods, every clearing, and humming insect is holy in the memory and experience of the red man. The white man's dead forget the country of their birth when they go walk among the stars. Our dead never forget this beautiful earth, for it is the mother of the red man. We are part of the earth and it is part of us. The perfumed flowers are our sisters; the deer, the horse, the great eagle, these are our brothers. The rocky crests, the juices of the meadows; the body heat of the pony, and man — all belong to the same family. So, when the Great Chief in Washington sends word that he wishes to buy our land, he asks much of us.

The Great Chief sends word he will reserve us a place so that we can live comfortably to ourselves. He will be our father and we will be his children. So we will consider your offer to buy our land. But it will not be easy. For this land is sacred to us. The shining water moves in the streams and you must remember that it is sacred, and you must teach your children that it is sacred and that each ghostly reflection in the clear water of the lake tells of events and memories in the life of my people.

The water's murmur is the voice of my father's father.

The rivers are our brothers, they quench our thirst. The rivers carry our canoe and feed our children. If we sell you our lands, you must remember, and teach your children that the rivers are our brothers, and yours, and you must henceforth give the rivers the kindness you would give any brother. The red man has always retreated before the advancing white man, as the mist of the mountains runs before the morning sun. But the ashes of our fathers are sacred. Their graves are holy ground, and so these hills, these trees, this portion of the earth is consecrated to us. We know that the white man does not understand our ways. One portion of land is the same to him as the next, for he is a stranger who comes in the night and takes from the land whatever he needs. The earth is not his brother, but his enemy, and when he has conquered it, he moves on. He leaves his father's graves behind, his father's graves and his childrens' birthright are forgotten. He treats his mother, the earth, and his brother, the sky, as things to be bought and leaves behind only a desert. I do not know. Our ways are different from your ways. The sight of your cities pains the eyes of the red man. But perhaps it is because the red man is a savage and does not understand.

There is no quiet place in the white man's cities. No place to hear the unfurling of leaves in spring or the rustle of insects wings. But perhaps it is because I am a savage and do not understand. The clatter only seems to insult the ears.

And what is there to life if a man cannot hear the lonely

cry of the whipporwill or the arguments of the frogs around a pond at night?

I am a red man and do not understand.

The Indian prefers the soft sound of the wind darting over the face of a pond, and the smell of the wind itself, cleansed by a midday rain or scented with the pinon pine. The air is precious to the red man, for all things share the same breath — the beasts, the trees, the man, they all share the same breath. The white man does not seem to notice the air he breaths. Like a man dying for many days, he is numb to the stench.

But if we will sell you our land, you must remember that the air is precious to us, that the air shares its spirit with all the life it supports. The wind that gave our grandfather his first breath also receives his last sigh. And the wind must also give our children the spirit of life. And if we sell you our land, you must keep it apart and sacred, as a place where even the white man can go to taste the wind that is sweetened by the meadow's flowers.

So we will consider your offer to buy our land. If we decide to accept, I will make one condition: the white man must treat the beasts of this land as his brothers. I am a savage and I do not understand how the smoking iron horse can be more important than the buffalo that we kill only to stay alive. What is man without the beasts? If all the beasts were gone, men would die from a great loneliness of spirit. For whatever happens to the beasts soon happens to man. All things are connected.

You must teach your children that the ground beneath their feet is the ashes of our grandfathers. So that they will respect the land, tell your children what we have taught our children, that the earth is our mother. Whatever befalls the earth befalls the sons of the earth. If men spit upon the ground, they spit upon themselves. This we know.

All things are connected like the blood which unites one family. All things are connected. Whatever befalls the earth befalls the sons of the earth. Man did not weave the web of life, he is merely a strand in it. Whatever he does to the web, he does to himself. But we will consider your offer to go to the reservation you have for my people. We will live apart and in peace. It matters little where we spend the rest of our days. Our children have seen their fathers humble in defeat. Our warriors have felt shame, and after defeat they turn their days in idleness and contaminate their bodies with sweet foods and strong drink. It matters little where we pass the rest of our days. They are not many. A few more hours, a few more winters, and none of the children of the great tribes that once lived on this earth or that roam now in small bands in the woods will be left to mourn the graves of a people once as powerful and as hopeful as yours. But why should I mourn the passing of my people? Tribes are made of men, nothing more. Men come and go, like the waves of the sea. Even the white man, whose God walks and talks with him as friend to friend, cannot be exempt from the common destiny. We may be brothers after all; we shall see. One thing we know, which white men may one day discover — our God is the same God. You may think now that you own Him as you wish to own our land, but you cannot.

He is the god of man and His compassion is equal for the red man and the white. This earth is precious to Him and to harm the earth is to heap contempt on its Creator.

The whites too shall pass; perhaps sooner than all other tribes.

Continue to contaminate your bed, and you will one night suffocate in your waste. But in your perishing you will shine brightly, fired by the strength of the God who brought you to this land and for some special purpose gave you dominion over this land and over the red man. That destiny is a mystery to us, for we do not understand when the buffalo are all slaughtered, the wild horses are tamed, the secret corners of the forest heavy with the scent of many men and the view of the ripe hills blotted by talking wires.

Where is the thicket? Gone. Where is the eagle? Gone.

And what is it to say good-bye to the swift pony and the

hunt? So we will consider your offer to buy our land. If we agree it will be to secure the reservation you have promised. There, perhaps, we may live our brief days as we wish. When the last red man has vanished from this earth, and his memory is only the shadow of a cloud moving across the prairie, these shores and forests will still hold the spirits of my people.

For they love this earth as the new-born loves its mother's heartbeat.

So if we sell you land, love it as we've loved it. Care for it as we've cared for it. Hold in your mind the memory of the land as it is when you take it. And with all your strength, with all your mind, and with all your heart, preserve it for your children and love it . . . as God loves us all.

One thing we know. Our God is the same God. This earth is precious to Him.

Even the white man cannot be exempt from the common destiny.

We may be brothers after all. We shall see.